Celebrating the Seasons

with children

festivals, crafts, seasonal songs,
recipes and stories

written and illustrated by
Helen Royall

Earth Spirit Publications

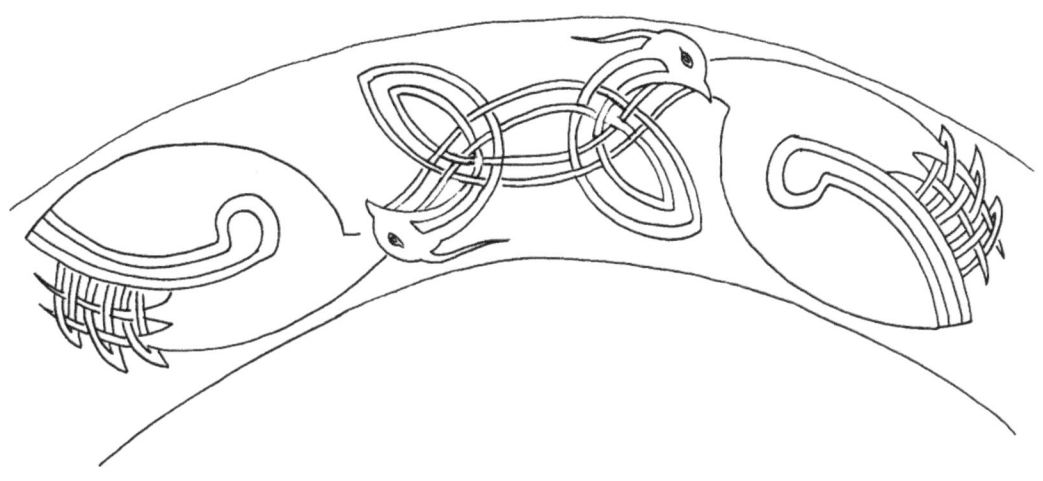

Published by Earth Spirit Publications

ISBN 978-0-9561500-0-4

CONTENTS

ACKNOWLEDGEMENTS

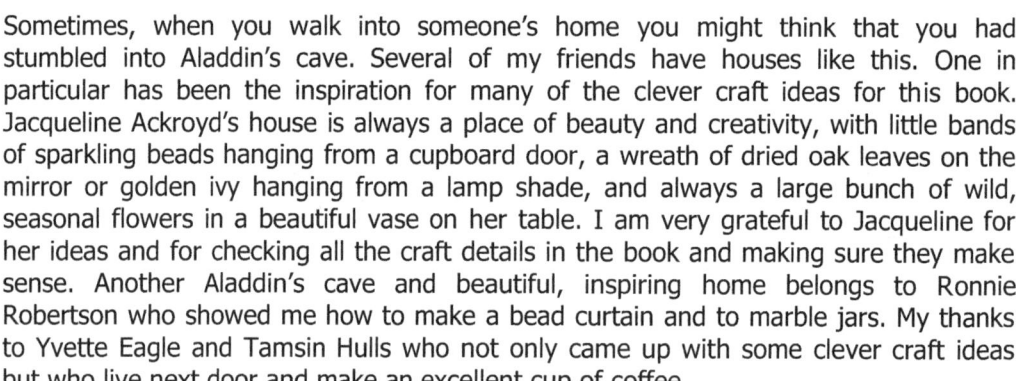

Sometimes, when you walk into someone's home you might think that you had stumbled into Aladdin's cave. Several of my friends have houses like this. One in particular has been the inspiration for many of the clever craft ideas for this book. Jacqueline Ackroyd's house is always a place of beauty and creativity, with little bands of sparkling beads hanging from a cupboard door, a wreath of dried oak leaves on the mirror or golden ivy hanging from a lamp shade, and always a large bunch of wild, seasonal flowers in a beautiful vase on her table. I am very grateful to Jacqueline for her ideas and for checking all the craft details in the book and making sure they make sense. Another Aladdin's cave and beautiful, inspiring home belongs to Ronnie Robertson who showed me how to make a bead curtain and to marble jars. My thanks to Yvette Eagle and Tamsin Hulls who not only came up with some clever craft ideas but who live next door and make an excellent cup of coffee.

Another home that I love to visit, this time because, when you walk through the front door you feel like you have walked into the garden, belongs to my friend Rae Wood. She always tries to encourage me to go out of doors to enjoy nature and has a wide knowledge of the things we may encounter. My thanks to Rae who checked the nature ideas and came up with the wonderful Wheel of Activities. And my thanks to Jenny Watson who helped with ideas for outdoor activities and who lent me a laundry bag full of books to look through for reference. Also to Sandra Hosler who read over the early manuscript and encouraged me to continue. Sandra and Adam Hosler thought through many of the outdoor activities with me.

Anna Gelgyn not only has a beautiful home but also helps other people to make their home a place of peace and beauty. She came up with ideas for ritual and continues to celebrate the seasons with her friends and family.

My thanks go to my friend Lesley Collins who lived and celebrated the seasons while her children were growing up and with whom I tried many of the ideas over the years. Lesley would often tell me a story about things that she had done or had seen done and I couldn't wait to get home to try them. Also for my friend Dianne Hydes who supported me and who particularly liked the stories.

My cousin and friend Penny Goode has much experience with allergies and has experimented with wonderful recipes and invited us round for the most delicious meals. My thanks to her for some of the recipe ideas.

To my dearest friend Ruth Mantin my thanks for being there throughout and supporting me, and for contributing to and checking the chapter on Goddesses, and to her family for putting up with me bringing the paperwork to their home whenever I visited.

Stories write themselves I've heard but these have been helped along by talking them through with friends. For lending me a little of their magic my thanks to Alexander Mackenzie, Peter Morris, Maureen Amelia Brodie, Ruth Mantin, Naomi Mantin, Graham Harvey and Jan Wood.

Graham Harvey checked my ideas and stories throughout and kept me, not so much on the 'straight and narrow' as the 'accurate but creative'. I am very grateful to him for his clarity and support.

My creativity is much better than my grammar and so I am very grateful to John Parsons who carefully checked the manuscript through, and to Richard Lamb who checked some early drafts and surprised himself by adding some ideas.

My approach to writing this book has been very much influenced by John Seymour (NLP) whose clarity and perception helped me to stay positive and clear in my intent. I have used many of his ideas in my own life and in my relationship with my daughter and I have included some of those ideas in the book.

My thanks also go to my family for their support and encouragement. To my sister Jane who sat down with my rough idea several years ago and supported me all the way, my brother Geoff, a brilliant cartoonist, who offered to help with illustrations whenever I needed it and to my brother Pip who suffered the slings and arrows of living with a writer (mainly in the form of no washing up for days).

The music seemed like a good idea at the time but I am grateful to Peter Timms for making sure that the rounds fit together and for finding time in his busy schedule to check for musical grammatical errors and to Marion Donovan who used her magic machine to transcribe them.

Of course none of this would have happened if it hadn't been for my wonderful daughter Ruth. To her I dedicate the book and look forward to many more happy seasons together.

FOREWORD

Stories hold the world together and keep it going around. At least, this is true when people tell the stories to each other. We have inherited a vast warehouse of stories from our ancestors and been given even more by our neighbours in other cultures. Some of these stories are 'just for fun', others convey great wisdom, beauty and power. But the fun, wisdom, beauty and power are locked away until someone tells the stories and someone hears them. When story-tellers do their job well, their hearers are inspired to go and tell the story to someone else. So the story grows, flourishes, blooms and bears fruit in yet more power, beauty, wisdom and fun. It might change, sometimes it has to change, but so does everything that lives. Perhaps each telling of the story gets closer to its real version rather than further away.

Helen Royall is a story-teller who loves the stories she tells. She has obviously cherished them and has, therefore, been rewarded by being gifted to tell them with considerable grace and inspiration. She has not left her store of wisdom closed and hidden and private, but brings out riches to share and be shared.

In this book she does not share only the riches of stories told by humans, generation to generation, neighbour to neighbour, or culture to culture. Helen has listened to the stories told by the earth, by the land around her as it lives through its growing seasons. So, here she shares ways of celebrating seasons and lives in a rich community of life. She offers guidance on making things that celebrate the world in which we live, and thereby participating in the story-telling of a world full of tales to be told.

The great tale of the round of seasons — Winter, Spring, Summer, Autumn and round again — each includes further stories and activities in which we might find our lives to be more meaningful, more enjoyable and certainly more full of company. It would, of course, be possible to begin the journey around the seasons at any point. This is just as well, it means that whenever you read this book you can go straight to the stories and craft ideas relevant to that season. If you are planning a party you might find material here that will inspire you to link some event in your family (a birthday or an anniversary perhaps) with whatever is happening seasonally in the tale the earth is telling.

Helen re-tells tales told centuries ago. Many people today are finding rich resonances with the ways in which seasons were celebrated in Celtic times. They honour the old and ever new festivals of Samhaine, Imbolc, Beltaine and Lughnasad. Many people again celebrate the solstices and equinoxes that mark the middle of seasons in Europe (although in North America they are thought of as the beginning of seasons). It doesn't really matter what you call yourself, or what you call these festivals and seasons. Or, rather, there are lots of perfectly good stories to be told about yourself and your celebrations and what's happening in the world around you. Certainly, this book does not constrain anyone to do what the author does, think as she does, or follow everything she suggests.

She provides some inspiration and encouragement, some first steps. The way she tells these stories is not always the way they have been told before. She does not pretend that these are exactly the words of our ancestors. Instead, she invites us to hear ancient stories in new ways, for new times. So, this book can be read by Pagans and Christians, Humanists and Buddhists and anyone else who wants to be enchanted and inspired. They can be read by parents and children, teachers and pupils, or by any style of adults or youth. They make it easy to see how the grand themes told by the earth in her turning seasons can be enjoyed in simple ways in our own homes.

Some will want to go and build a bonfire in winter; others will be satisfied with candle light in the warmth of their kitchens. Some will want to re-tell the epics loved by our ancestors, others will be happy to acknowledge the names and key events of inspiring and exciting tales.

Some will want to acknowledge the changes in their bodies — or those of their growing children — in festivities and with presents. Others will be more private. But here are the resources to inspire greater confidence in being at home in the world, at home with those you love, and at home with yourself.

The seasons and the Goddesses and Gods honoured by our ancestors are continuously relevant to the age in which we live. Once you get to know them, they are very ordinary, very natural and very engaging. They connect you with the world around you far more than most newspapers. They make it easier to see the importance of treating the world and yourself with reverence and respect. They also make this so much more natural, and not at all mystical and otherworldly. But if they are 'just stories' that is good too, as long as they are good stories. Here, they are, ready for the telling and the doing.

This book should be very useful in the nurturance of children and their spirituality. It could be the foundation for a whole curriculum of studies. And the most wonderful thing is that you need never notice that you are learning! All the hard work of discovering the world and its stories and seasons is wrapped up in the fun of making, doing, giving, listening and telling. Adults, too, will be nurtured in the telling, listening, giving and doing. Perhaps, in fact, adults don't listen enough, and perhaps children's tales aren't told enough. Certainly the stories of the land, the seasons and the earth are not listened to with anything like adequate attention. For all these reasons, and more that you will discover, this book is a great gift and we should be enormously grateful to Helen Royall for sharing it with us.

Graham Harvey
Lecturer and researcher, Open University, UK
Author of *Listening People, Speaking Earth: Contemporary Paganism*.

INTRODUCTION

> *"Others ... have heard a wilder music, playing to an older beat, and wish to reunite with Mother Nature ...under the light of the stars and changing moonlight, in a simpler way."*
>
> 'A Witch Alone'. Marian Green

After years of neglect and persecution, change and development the Old Ways still draw us to celebrate and care for Mother Earth. Wonder begins to creep back into the hearts and minds of our children and the magic of Mother Nature calls us to respond and sway with the cycles of the year. Ancient nature traditions and celebrations are echoed in our play and in many of the festivals celebrated throughout the year and children begin to question a culture that lives on the edge of virtual reality. Old traditions and knowledge that have their roots deep in the heart of the Celtic Islands gently guide us towards an understanding and love of the natural rhythm of each year. More and more families turn away from a world full of instant gratification and synthetic sustenance, religions that have lost the sense of the numinous and education that no longer encourages imagination.

When my daughter was born I knew that I wanted to give her the opportunity of experiencing a more nature based spiritual pathway. I could find very few books at that time that gave me the myths, legends and cultural stories that I thought would help her. Stories told how the Goddess was controlled, abducted or tortured and children's songs echoed a patriarchy that I did not want to encourage. For a long time it felt like we were swimming up stream and my daughter was uncomfortable being different, but gradually she realised that she had a choice and that her own imagination and learning were being encouraged all the time. Now she is a creative, wholesome and independent young person who happily discovers her own magic and cares about Nature and the world she lives in.

As people again become comfortable with an older terminology, celebrating the Winter Solstice as well as Christmas and having Beltaine gatherings as well as May Day holidays, the deep, ancient voice of the Celtic Islands is heard again drawing us to a care and guardianship of nature's cycles and wilder ways.

It is often disconcerting to find that it is not warm and sunny in summer or cold and frosty in winter; it is possible to eat strawberries in January and walk into shops selling Christmas decorations and cards in September, but when we truly sit within the season we are able to appreciate fully it's nature and enjoy more appropriate activities as a result.

Over the years my family have gathered ideas and traditions that help us to do just that and to celebrate and make sense of the cycle of festivals and holidays. We try to keep specific activities for certain parts of the year so that each season can be fully appreciated.

This book is not about setting down any rules – I've made up many of my ideas as I've gone along – it is a pot of suggestions to dip in to, it is suggested directions, a bouquet of colourful ideas.

Be free, be joyous and get in touch with your wild side as you live through each season, staying firmly rooted in Mother Earth, sharing her richness and generosity, stillness and calm, her wildness and warmth. With thankful hearts receive and give back your own harvest.

THE GODDESS AND THE CYCLE OF THE YEAR

> *"...the Goddess is the power of intelligent embodied love that is the ground of all being. The earth is the body of the Goddess. All beings are interdependent in the web of life. Nature is intelligent, alive and aware."*
>
> 'Rebirth of the Goddess'. Carol Christ

The Nature Festivals

There are four ancient fire festivals, **Samhaine** (pronounced Sow-in), **Imbolc** (pronounced Imelc), **Beltaine** and **Lammas** or **Lughnasad** (pronounced Lunassa). In the days before written calendars Samhaine would have come on the first hoar frost, Imbolc with the thaw, Beltaine when the hawthorn blossomed and Lammas with the cutting of the first sheaf of corn. Later the solar rites were added - Spring and Autumnal Equinox and Summer and Winter Solstice.

To our ancestors every part of the year had its tasks, its efforts and its harvests. From the earliest known religious activities of humankind upon Earth, offerings, rituals, celebrations and acts of propitiation seem to have been made to Mother Earth. The oldest festivals seem to be the winter ones as people were probably working too hard in summer to find time to gather and celebrate. Before clocks and calendars Mother Nature would instruct the people what to do and at what time.

With song and dance, mime and words the people in their community would act out the stories of the Old Ones and trace the cycle of the seasons, of Life and Death. Parts would be chosen by lot, with symbols baked in a cake or hidden in a bag. Dancers would join hands in a circle and games would be played.

Celebratory food would be shared and the whole community would be present and counted.

As time moves on an organic process occurs as festivals are forgotten, different religious rituals intermingle and grow, and new ideas and celebrations are added to the old.

The seasons are not so easily marked with the development of modern agriculture and the movement further and further away from the natural tides of nature. Sometimes our bodies miss the changing seasons as they become accustomed to central heating, cars and television, food from supermarkets out of season and efficient electric lighting.

The old festivals have been given a time in the calendar which helps us mark the turning of the tides but for some these dates mean very little and the festivals are celebrated when it seems appropriate. The seasons of the earth correspond with our own bodies' seasons and it is good to mark each turn with quietness or celebration, lone walks or shared rituals, contemplation or discussion.

Even though we may not be able to involve the whole community it is possible to celebrate as a family. Often friends want to share in celebrating the season and experiencing the richness of appropriate seasonal activities.

Each season beckons us and teaches us to understand the Earth's cycles and to respond from within our own hearts in celebration and joy and deep reverence. Pre-Christian Celtic people worked out the passage of time in moon phases. Why not go outside and see what phase the moon is in and try to work out what season you are in? How does that make you feel? What seasonal tasks need to be done? How can you give thanks and celebrate it?

The Goddess

Concepts of the Goddess differ from person to person and have shifted slightly even over the short time that people have discovered and re-discovered thealogy. For some she is real and external and for others she is internal and contingent on one's own state of being, and for some she is both, as Starhawk says, "She exists and we create her".

Carol Christ, who has made an important and distinctive contribution to thealogy, expresses it in the preface of her book 'Rebirth of the Goddess',
"For me and for many others, finding the Goddess has felt like coming home to a vision of life that we have always known deeply within ourselves, that we are part of nature and that our destiny is to participate fully in the cycles of birth, death and renewal that characterise life on the earth."

The Goddess is the living earth. Everything is alive and part of her body, minerals, trees and plants, even crystals and mountains. All of us are part of her and all are important and sacred.

In our family we choose to include the Goddess in our celebrations and have found many delightful ways of doing this, as this book will show.

The Goddess and the Cycle of the Year

The moon comes in four phases – waxing, full, waning and dark. The Great Goddess, Mother Earth, follows this pattern in her seasons of Maiden as she is young and full of life; Mother as she is betrothed to her beloved and gives birth; and Crone as she becomes old and wise and her consort is cut down at harvest, leaving her with the seed of the new child, the new cycle. Her Dark Time follows this as she goes underground to await quietly the birth of her son at Winter Solstice. For some this time represents death, when we move into the Summerland of Avalon, the Celtic heaven where trees bear both flowers and fruit simultaneously. This is a magical place where the soul can rest and meditate on all it has learned in its life on Earth. Contemporary Pagan mythology is typically structured by the relationship of the Goddess and her consort/son, the Horned God. The Goddess gives birth to him in mid-winter, marries him at the beginning of summer and sacrifices him to herself in autumn, ensuring the fertility of the coming year.

Like the moon cycle, the seasonal cycle is a powerful way to experience the processes of birth, growth, death and birth. The four phases correspond with the four seasons – Imbolc, springtime, when new life is all around; Beltaine, summer, when the earth is full and luscious; Lammas, autumn, when we reap the harvest and Samhaine, winter, when we make time for ourselves to be quiet and ponder all that has passed and all the wonderful possibilities that might be to come and we prepare our celebrations for the return of the Goddess. For some the Goddess is complete alone and does not need a God or consort in order to create the new life within and around her.

In our family, to represent this changing cycle we have our Mother Earth 'act out' the parts for us in the Nature Garden. We also include other representations - Lady Spring takes the place of Mother Earth at Eostar and the Corn Maiden at Lammas.

The four aspects of the Goddess were often represented as three - as the three that were visible. This triple aspect, maiden, mother and crone (Greek: Hebe-Hera-Hecate) were to be replaced by the all male trinities such as the Germanic Pagan trinity of Woden, Thor and Saxnot and the Christian Father, Son and Holy Spirit.

For some, as well as the Great Goddess, (who is a representation of the Universal Energy, Great Spirit etc.) there are other Goddesses who represent aspects of the one Goddess. Objects, colours, fragrances, blessings, rituals and prayers can represent these Goddesses at any time of the year. Some examples are listed below.

To write about traditions in an essentially mythogenic culture is difficult, as contemporary Paganism and Celtic spirituality are creating myths and rituals as they go along. Starhawk in her book 'The Spiral Dance' says we value the courage to take risks, to make mistakes, to be our own authorities. A contemporary Celtic pathway "must validate us in discovering and sharing our experiences, inner and outer. Its goal should be that impossible task of teaching ourselves – because we have no models and no teachers who can show us the way – to become human, fully alive with all the human passions and desires, faults and limitations, and infinite possibilities." Thealogy states that the religious images of our dominant cultures have presented the divine as immutable, eternal, unchanging, whereas these earth-based spiritualities recognise the sacred in the process of change and flux.

More important then, than representing the Goddess, is the act of 'Goddessing'. This is when we do things that are by nature part of the Goddess – acts of thoughtfulness, kindness, and compassion. Acts that are life giving, life-enhancing, that care for the earth and other people, acts that show that we honour ourselves, others and the earth.

The Nature Table

This is a place where you can reflect the season and follow the cycle of the year. It helps us to focus on what is happening and is a lovely place to put the things we might collect that season. It is a good idea to have several boxes, one for each season and one for each festival, and to put things in that will be used each year, such as coloured cloths, little models of animals, pixies, and fairies. You can also collect pictures for the wall or postcards, and if you use aromatherapy oils or Joss-sticks you might want to use special ones for the different times of year.

Children appreciate watching the seasons turning in a nature table or nature corner. As the colours change and different things are collected the nature table reflects the changing patterns that are all around us.

We try to be careful not to gather handfuls of living flowers or to keep insects or animals that could be free. Sometimes it feels okay to gather wild flowers that are growing in abundance and would benefit from a little culling, or flowers from the garden that appreciate some thinning out. We also like to arrange twigs and branches that have fallen from trees that show us the season very clearly.

As time has gone on we have collected a selection of beautifully shaped logs. One came from a river, washed clean and smooth, one from a forest with lots of interesting holes and surfaces, one in the shape of an owl, another a thick piece of honeysuckle. Each time we change season we change the piece of wood that acts as the shape to build the display around.

I include a representation of earth, air, fire and water, the four elements of life. For example crystals, stones, earth in potted plants flowers or sand for earth; Joss-sticks or things hanging like a tiny kite for air; candles or pictures of the sun for fire; water, wine, or mirrors for water.

Here are some of the ideas we have tried. I have made a Mother Earth and she has several different cloaks and shawls, which change through the year.

Samhaine

Our nature table at Samhaine might have photographs or reminders of the past year, or a picture of anyone who has died in the year and any poems for them or flowers or some other symbol of gratitude. We put ochre, orange and moss green cloths on the table, sometimes burn frankincense, and gradually collect things from our walks or which we have made. Sometimes we might add a black cloth for the festival itself. Mother Earth (a little hand made doll like an old woman) puts on a warm cloak or shawl and carries a basket to go wooding so that she can have a warm fire when she gets home. Sometimes we put a candle on the table and light it at night when we light the candle on our dining table and sometimes we light it when we tell stories in the evening or to welcome guests. During December we heat orange and cinnamon oil on a little burner in the tableau and Mother Earth wears her warm velvet cloak. The table would then be cleared and a few sparkly cloths or a shiny pale blue one laid out ready for the December presents. Mother Earth has a special crown for Yule.

At the Winter Solstice we hang a beautiful glass sun (given to us by Ruth, a good friend who enjoys our seasonal decorations) above our table to show that the days will begin to get longer. We decorate the whole house as well as the Nature Table during Yule and then clear away again in January and cover the table with a white cloth and make decorations like snowflakes and glitter sticks and a family of gnomes carrying lanterns and dried seeds.

Imbolc

As the season turns with the thaw and new life is seen in the form of the pale nodding heads of the snowdrops, our table adds a dark brown cloth under the white to represent this, and a pot of snowdrops appears (if we remembered to prepare one!). We find lots of white things to put on the table and Lady Spring joins the tableau. She has doves and baby rabbits around her. We choose some branches of a tree with new buds on if we can find one and watch as the tiny new leaves start to shoot. We make eyes of light for the Fire Goddess Brigit, celebrated at this time of year, and little blossoms and blossom fairies, then gradually add our decorated eggs as spring creeps on and Eostar is celebrated.

At Eostar our cloths change to fresh lemon and spring green. Lady Spring wears a crown of flowers and has a beautiful white hare at her feet. She wears a white cloak (like Persephone rising from the underworld) and we add pots of spring flowers. We have saved one decorated egg from each year and hang these from decorated branches that hang from the ceiling. We often have hyacinths instead of burning oils or Joss sticks.

Beltaine

Now a Maypole appears and we use little figures from my daughter's dolls house to dance around the foot of it. The cloths change to rich green or bright yellow and we use an old honey pot in the shape of a beehive, which was given to us by Peter, a friend who loved the local honey, to tempt our alder cone bees and we add vases of wild flowers and grasses. Lady Spring disappears and Mother Earth takes off her shawl and bonnet and puts on a fresh white apron. Her little basket is filled with tissue paper flowers. As summer moves on we fill our table with things from our holidays or walks and sometimes put postcards from friends in. At Summer Solstice we might burn jasmine or geranium oil and we change our sun for a moon to show that the days will begin to shorten.

Lammas

At Lammas a bright red cloth can be added and Mother Earth is replaced with a corn doll. This year I used a bright yellow cloth for the summer that was passing and a deep gold cloth for the gold of autumn.

On the table I had shells from summer holidays and golden crystals to prepare for autumn, and gold glitter for the beauty and warmth of the sunlit evenings. Sometimes we put a vase of corn and poppies on the table and add fruit and berries as the season continues, and sometimes, if we make special loaves, we put a small one on the table. Our crystals turn golden and yellow and we might burn Ylang Ylang or lavender. We are less likely to burn incense and oils at this time of year because our house usually smells of wonderful cooking. At the Autumn Equinox we add a bowl of clear spring water and make a beautiful arrangement of fruit and berries. We may add some herbs as an offering to Hecete.

Other Areas

As well as a nature corner we have a small seasonal decoration on our dinning table, or sometimes just a candle that we light at every meal. We say a blessing before we eat and extinguish the candle using a snuffer at the end of the meal. We also have an altar, which has a simple arrangement of earth, air, fire and water, and a seasonal coloured cloth covering. It is used for rituals and meditation. We try to end our day with meditation but we don't always manage it!

RITES AND RITUALS

> "*The Goddess awakes in infinite forms and a thousand disguises. She is found where She is least expected, appears out of nowhere and everywhere to illuminate the open heart. She is singing ... to us: to be awake, to commit ourselves to life, to be a lover in the world and of the world, to join our voices in the single song of constant change and creation. For Her law is love unto all beings, and She is the cup of the drink of life.*"
>
> '*The Spiral Dance*'. Starhawk

As the cycle of the year unfolds we are drawn to be watchful, to take part and to celebrate. Each unfolding moment is precious and is part of an infinite picture.

When we recognise that a moment is remarkable or sacred, we often wish to mark it somehow. This is ritual.

Ritual can be simple or involved. It can be the lighting of a candle; a simple word or it can be the gathering of many people to perform complicated and intricate patterns of movement and poetry.

On our dining table we have a small seasonal arrangement and at meal times we light a candle and say or sing a simple blessing to remind us that the act of eating and sharing food is sacred and delightful. We try to make the act of coming together for a meal a pleasurable gathering and sharing time. We may not always achieve this but it is something for which we feel it is worth striving. When we have friends who follow a different spiritual pathway than our own we enjoy sharing different blessings.

Birthdays are a real treat and something we all look forward to. We try to recognise how special the birthday person is and decorate their chair the night before in brightly coloured, sparkly cloths. We lay out a breakfast table and pile up presents around their place. We wrap up lots of little presents and save all the birthday cards that may have arrived a few days early to be opened on the day. The birthday person comes down to a wonderful arrangement and usually gets his or her favourite breakfast, which everyone else enjoys as well. On my brother's fiftieth birthday, we managed to wrap up fifty presents for him. These included a lot of miniature bars of chocolate but the table looked very bright and overflowing with gifts. My friend, Lesley, remembers when her daughter had a birthday when she was at kindergarten. The teacher asked Lesley about her daughter's birth and on Nicky's birthday, the teacher told everyone the story of Nicky and how she came into the world on her birthday. The teacher included some special presents Nicky got so that her family remembered how she had been brought into the world and how her brother was eagerly awaiting her arrival. Lesley remembered the look on Nicky's face and how moved everyone was. I remember being asked to tell a story for a friend's 40th birthday. I asked all his family and friends to try to remember any thing they could that had happened to him and on the day told the story of his life so far. He was astounded, not just with the surprise party but with how much I seemed to know about him! We laughed a great deal and the party was a great success.

Any ceremony or ritual that tells a person that they are welcome and important is an essential ingredient to their understanding of who they are.

Rituals can be part of everyday life, adding that sense of 'other', of sacredness, of moments set aside or captured in our memory. Rituals help us to make sense of our world and honour it. Rituals to mark the phases of the moon, stages of a relationship, times of the year, times of day, family events or times, friendships and many, many others. Rituals give us rhythm and slow us down in the ever-increasing speed of life; they give us honour and respect for our life styles and each other. They can also help us to create things in our life that we most desire. My friend Anna, when she was in a situation that was making her very unhappy, bought a beautiful butterfly mug. Butterflies represent freedom and change to her and every time she drank from her mug she felt she was moving towards that freedom and away from the unhappy situation.

Rituals can also be large group events, marking important times and occasions. When these rituals grow out of the experiences and emotions of the group members themselves, they are meaningful and organic. They can be complicated or simple and help those taking part to move to a deeper level of awareness. They can be scripted, guided or created as they happen and each ritual will have a life of its own and a different meaning and depth for each person taking part. Our Winter Solstice celebrations have become a ritual that grew out of repeated activities year after year.

Rites of passage are also important in our lives. Some are easier to mark than others. A rite of passage marks the movement from one place in our lives to another, from one stage to another, for example when a girl becomes a woman with the onset of menstruation. It is harder to recognise a specific occasion for a boy but it is well worth thinking of ways to acknowledge his move from childhood to adulthood.

When my daughter was born I bought her a bracelet and added a scorpion charm to it (her birth sign). As she grows up, I add a charm for any important or memorable event in her life. She has an engraved card for her fifth birthday, a candle for when she was in bed with the measles and coped with them so well. We discussed the fact that 7 was a good age to get the measles and that it was helping her system to clear out all the unwanted toxins from her body. When she recovered, she seemed to have matured slightly and grown into the next stage of her life. On her eighteenth birthday I gave her the charm bracelet as her coming of age present. She chose that age as the right one for her to receive it.

I also had a beautiful Goddess necklace for her, which is a smaller version of the one I usually wear. It is a figure of a woman/Goddess holding a jewel (the world or the moon perhaps). Mine is a moonstone; my daughter's is a little red jewel in the shape of a teardrop, or possibly a drop of blood. I gave this to her when she started menstruating. Her best friend, Naomi, got the same so it was an experience they could share. When Nicky became a woman she was very excited and rang her best friend to tell her. I was very privileged to be there that day and we had a special meal to celebrate. Her mother arranged a little party for her and her friends to celebrate and I was invited to come and tell my Pandora stories – a series of Goddess centred creation stories. Since then Nicky looks forward to her periods as something she is proud of and happy with. They are part of her womanhood.

It can be difficult to know what to do for boys but it is important to follow them and let your relationship with them guide you.

One friend of mine, Dianne, suggested that she would buy her son a beautiful razor and shaving brush set.

Another friend, Sandra, wrote her son a letter in the form of a story to convey how much she had enjoyed being part of his childhood and how it had been a privilege to watch him grow through the years.

Another ritual that I enjoy with my daughter is meditation. I often guide these, as she likes me to. We have done some work on meeting our angels and Ruth has a guardian angel called Ellen. One evening she was feeling particularly worried. She had experienced something that was very difficult to handle and it will probably always affect her in some way but she has handled it very well so far. When we did a meditation one evening, I suggested that she ask her angel to help her with the things that were worrying her. She went into the meditation and when she came out she told me what had happened. She went to a place where many angels lived in little houses. At first, it seemed empty and then a group of angels burst out of their windows and doors. Out of the biggest house came a figure that looked like death without his scythe. He was rather frightening. The angels covered him over with a large golden bubble and it floated upwards with this figure in it. The angels then pointed to the bubble, it burst, and the frightening figure was gone. Ruth sometimes uses this image to help her when she is worried. She puts the worrying thing into a big golden bubble and lets it float up into the air and then bursts it.

Another ritual we have enjoyed is a Moon Gathering. This is a time when women gather on a certain phase of the moon – be it new, waxing, full or waning. We gather to share together our lives and the things that are happening to us. For some, the time of the waxing moon is a time to focus on the things that we are taking on or wish to take on. The time of the waning moon is a time to let go of things and the full moon is a time to simply be and enjoy. Some people suggest that the full moon is not a good time to share magic – if magic is something that you are interested in. This is because the moon at that time is neither waxing nor waning, it is simply being still, so we gather together to eat lots (as with many gatherings!) and enjoy each other's company.

Although this may not seem to be a rite or a ritual, many people who follow on this pathway believe that it is very empowering to keep a journal. This can take any form you like. Mine is brief, one side of A5, and I usually write it when things are not going too well and I want to change things.

The other sort of journal I keep from time to time is one for my wish list. I use a large, brightly coloured book and write in it in beautiful coloured pens. I often illustrate it with coloured borders and patterns. I write down my vision for me. I then write down what I need to do now to move towards it. I love writing in this book and tend to write in it at the change of season.

The other sort of journal can be for spells and workings that you wish to record, or for a general record of things. Of course, you can combine all these different journals if you enjoy keeping a record of how you are doing. In the first season, Samhaine, you can see other ideas for ways of recording your year.

ACTIVITY WHEEL OF THE YEAR

★ local map ~ mark useful trees & bushes

★ dry herbs ~ pot pourée, food, moth repellant

★ garden pruning ~ look for different colours e.g. red/yellow dogwood

★ storage system ~ for drying & storing plant materials

★ storing ~ leave in air to dry then in airtight container to stop colours fading

★ pussy willow ~ leave in jar or vase with no water, to dry

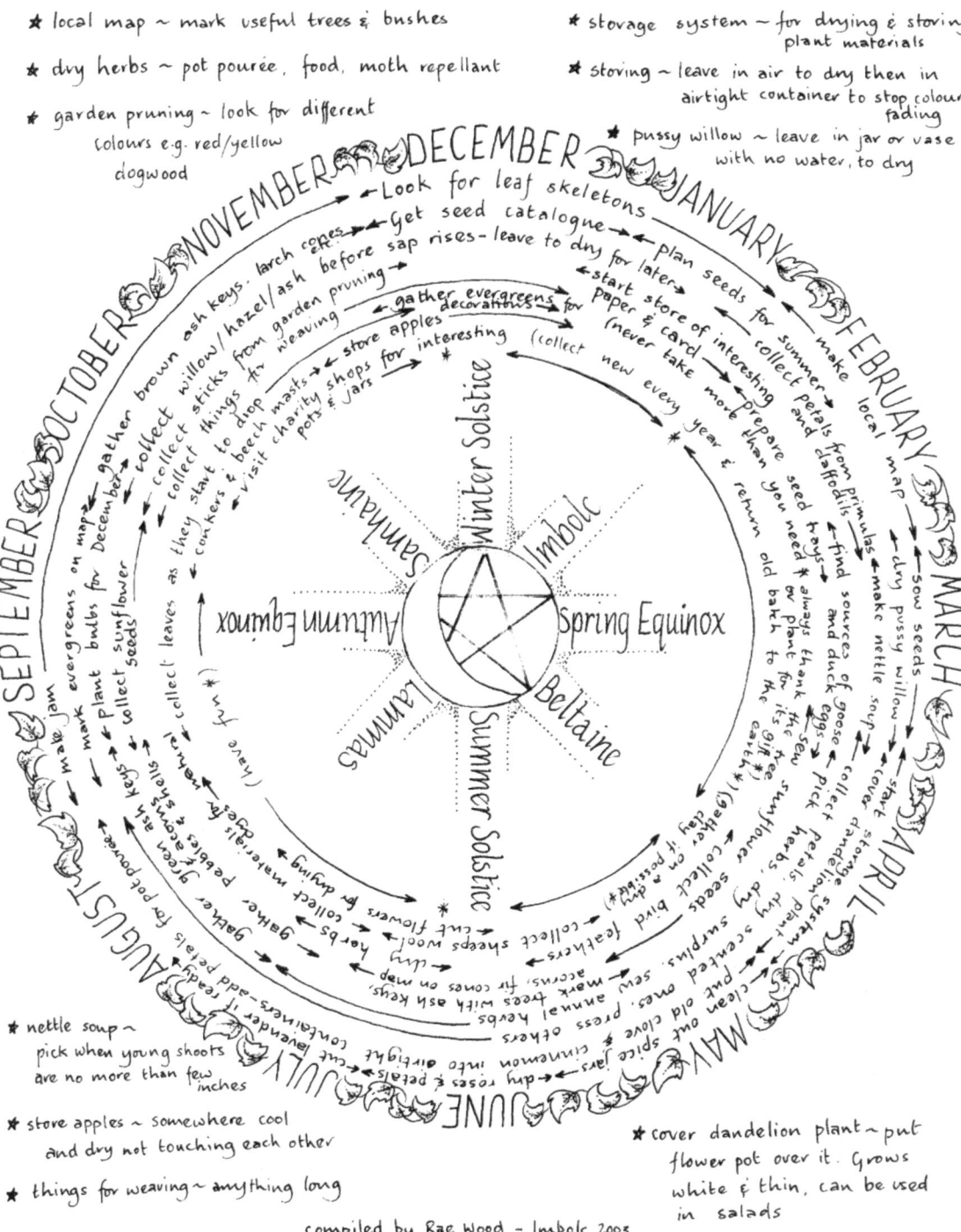

★ nettle soup ~ pick when young shoots are no more than few inches

★ store apples ~ somewhere cool and dry not touching each other

★ things for weaving ~ anything long

★ cover dandelion plant ~ put flower pot over it. Grows white & thin, can be used in salads

compiled by Rae Wood ~ Imbolc 2003

11

Samhaine

Clearing Out

SAMHAINE
(Pronounced Sow-in)
(31st October)

Samhaine, or Halloween, marks the beginning and the end of the year when Mother Earth rests to gather her strength for the turning tides of nature, affirming rebirth in the midst of darkness. As the leaves begin to fall, and the nights are long, this is the time to gather together to hear the old stories. The Celts called it Samhaine, which means 'summer's end', according to their ancient two-fold division of the year, when summer ran from Beltaine to Samhaine and winter ran from Samhaine to Beltaine.

Samhaine was the time of the slaughter, and preservation in salt, of livestock for winter meat and for the selection of the fittest animals for future breeding. Some suggest an earlier explanation of Samhaine that refers to a time when the Shamans would enter the Realms of the Dead at the first frosts, to conduct the souls of the recently departed to their place of rest, and to bring back knowledge and enlightenment. Many of our myths reflect this image and are good to tell at this time of year when the nights draw in.

 To those who celebrate this time, Samhaine is one of the four High Holidays, Greater Sabbats, or cross-quarter days. Because it is the most important holiday of the year, it is sometimes called 'THE Great Sabbat.' With such an important holiday, some people often hold two distinct celebrations. For some Samhaine is a time for one of the more serious rituals and children are not always invited, but adaptations can be made and children can be made welcome. Since my daughter has been old enough we have celebrated Samhaine with children.

Bobbing for apples is one activity popular at this time of year. This may well represent the remnants of a Pagan 'baptism' rite called a 'seining', according to some. The water-filled tub is a latter-day Cauldron of Regeneration, into which the novice's head is immersed. The custom of dressing in costume and 'trick-or-treating', not just by children, is of Celtic origin with survivals particularly strong in Scotland. In ancient times, roving bands would sing seasonal carols from house to house, making the tradition very similar to Yuletide wassailing.

At this time of year we like to mark the festival with a gathering of friends around a fire - outdoors if weather permits. Here are some of the ideas I have used successfully: we sometimes use two candles to mark the passing of the year, a black one for the old year and white for the new. A simple way is to light the black candle and let it burn away completely. While this happens we write on pieces of paper anything that we do not want to take forward into the New Year with us; for example any negative thoughts or beliefs we might have, or anything we might have done that we wished we could do differently. We don't tell anyone what these are. We then throw them on the fire and let them burn. One of us will read something appropriate about the turning of the year or we will tell a seasonal story. When the candle has burned down we light the white candle and write on pieces of paper things that we want to take forward into the New Year. We keep these pieces of paper and take them home with us.

Then it is time to eat together and share seasonal food and drink, for example apple and honey cakes, oatcakes and cider. Plenty of vegetables in a stew can be enjoyed and fruit salad to celebrate the harvest.

One year our friend, Rae, asked us each to make a weaving of our experiences through the year. Those of us who remembered brought back a beautiful representation of our year and shared them with the group. They were far too beautiful to burn so they have been kept as a happy reminder of our Samhaine gathering.

In ancient time Samhaine was believed to be a time when the veil was thin between the world of the living and the world of the dead. The dead are our friends and family, our ancestors who gave us life. We call them our 'beloved dead'. Death is a natural part of life and one of the gifts of the Goddess.

Samhaine is a time to look back over the year and count our blessings, the time to get out our photographs and put them in albums or on a wall display, the time to ask 'what have we done for the garden?' 'What have we learned that helped us or made us happy?' This is the time when we clean our house from top to bottom to prepare for and welcome the ancestors, and my friend Rae leaves a place at her table for those dear ones who have died that year. It might be good to visit the family graves and do some brass rubbings. We have now got quite a long way with compiling our family tree and we put together a family album for my parents on their Golden Wedding Anniversary.

Goddess for Samhain

Cerridwen

As autumn gives way to winter Cerridwen sits at the doorway to the cave of the underworld. She is large, round and very old. Her eyes are all seeing, deep and dark as pools. She stirs a large cauldron into which all souls must return for regeneration and inspiration.

There are many stories of Cerridwen, Some are of the fierce underworld Goddess who takes life in order to give it back again, and some of the all-knowing Wise One who guides the souls of the dead to drink from her cauldron of rebirth and knowledge.

The name translates as 'crooked' or 'bent' but possibly the 'wen' stems from 'gwen' the meaning "fair", "beloved", "blessed", or "sacred". Known also as the Celtic goddess of rebirth, transformation, and inspiration, Cerridwen sits at the turning point of Lammas and Samhaine. Her symbols are the cauldron, spider webs and pigs.

THE PRINCESS AND THE DRAGON

High in a tower, just west of where the last star shines, there lived a princess.

She lived all alone and spent her days looking out of the one window where she could see the world below her. Big and beautiful and terrifying it was to her and the princess dreamed each day that a wonderful prince would come and rescue her. "How could that be," she thought to herself, "when the only person who comes to my tower is the old woman in my dreams?"

Each night when the princess lay sleeping she dreamed that an old woman would come to watch over her and tend to her needs. Often the old woman spoke to her in a strange language that filled the princess with joy and a sense of freedom. The words seemed to have been made in a great fire or on the wings of the wind and left the princess feeling content and happy. The princess loved to dream because always her dreams gave her company. The old woman taught her many things and when the princess woke up in the morning sometimes she would find gifts. She never stopped to think how things could appear for real after a dream in case the old woman stopped coming to her.

Many years the princess had lived in the tower, her golden hair had grown so long that it fell almost to the ground at her feet, and shone like the very sun itself. Her skin was soft and clear and her eyes, though sad, shone with the gentle light of the stars. If any had laid eyes on her they would have fallen in love with her at once. But none came to rescue her from her tower and the princess looked out of her window, in fear for the big outside world and in hope that one day...one day...

One bright, sunlit day when the sky filled with rainbows, a brave and handsome young man rode by the tower. The princess called down to him and the young man looked up into the eyes of the most beautiful woman he had ever seen.

The prince, yes he was a fine young prince, instantly fell in love with the princess and called back to her. "Are you the person I have heard singing from a tower in the sunlight?"
"Oh yes," cried the princess, I have been waiting for a prince to come and save me from this tower where I have been captive for so long."

"How could anyone be so cruel?" thought the prince, "I must save this young woman. All I need to do is find a way into the tower." All day he tried to find a way to climb the steep, smooth slope of the tower, until at last he had an idea. "I will climb the tree at the side of the tower and then you must jump out to me and I will catch you." The prince looked brave and strong and so the princess jumped into his arms and together they climbed down.

From the forest floor the world did not look so frightening and so the princess forgot her fears and went off to find her way with the prince.

Soon they came to a brook that could give them water and several trees that would be good for shelter. Here they sat and talked about their different lives. The prince had been given half his father's lands and many servants and all the gold he desired but all the prince ever wanted was to go off in search of dragons. Though he had never seen one the prince had a terrible fear of dragons but he would never admit this to anyone. He told his father that the land must be rid of dragons before he would settle down and rule over his part of the kingdom. And so he had taken his best sword and one of his father's horses and gone out on his quest. He was strong and generous and had made many friends on the way but always he thought he heard the sound of a woman singing somewhere in the great forest and so his steps had led him in the direction of the tower. "And now I know why," said the prince. "It was to find you and take you home with me."

The princess shone with happiness. All her dreams had come true and now she would be fulfilled. She told the prince of her life in the tower and how she could not get out until someone saved her. The prince smiled and was pleased. Then the princess told the prince of her dreams and how the old woman had come to her and watched over her. It was strange how things had been left for her in the mornings but she had never actually seen the old woman. "If things were left for you in the morning," said the prince angrily, "then the old woman must have known how to get in and out and it must be she who had locked you in." The princess looked uncertain but maybe he was right. "The old woman seemed to care for me but how could she leave me locked up in the tower so long?" she wondered.

That evening they lit a fire and sat close together and the prince watched the firelight catch the gold and bronze of the princess's hair. He had never before seen anyone look so beautiful and he knew his love for her would last forever. They clung together in the cold night, glad of the warmth of the fire and each other and they told stories to each other that they had heard when they were younger, the prince about dashing knights who were brave and strong and the princess about the sigh of the wind and the song of the stars that the old woman told her in her dreams.

As she spoke the prince suddenly moved away from her and stood up with a jerk. He pulled out his sword and, pointing it towards her asked in a voice that the princess had never heard before, "what language is this you speak?"

The princess had not realised that she was speaking the words that the old woman had taught her. "It is nothing but poetry or child's talk, come sit back down you are frightening me." But the prince looked more frightened and said through gritted teeth. "It is the language of dragons, therefore you must be a dragon and I must kill you! You tricked me with your beautiful looks and your sweet voice but you are evil and I will rid the world of evil!" He was shouting now and the princess was very afraid. What had made her prince speak to her in this way?

Suddenly the fire seemed to flare up and the flames reach the top of the trees around them. The prince was terrified, he would be engulfed in the flames and he would die. He flailed his sword around desperately jabbing at the flames and then his worst nightmare appeared before his eyes as an enormous dragon walked towards him. Its eyes looked straight at him as if it knew his name, his very soul, and fire and dreadful smoke gushed from its nostrils. The prince froze in horror, his arms dropping to his sides unable to lift his sword. The dragon looked at the prince and spoke in a voice that seemed to come from the very fires of death. He was so afraid that he put his hands over his ears and fell to his knees. But the dragon went on speaking and as it spoke the prince noticed that the words seemed to have been made in a great fire or on the wings of the wind and left him feeling content and happy. "How can this be," thought the prince, "when the dragon is so evil and I must kill it?" But instead of saying this he found himself saying the words that the princess had spoken and as he spoke them he saw the dragon bow down and lay its mighty head on the ground. The enormous front leg came forward so that the prince and princess could climb up.

"No, no!" shouted the prince, "it is a trick. Everyone knows that dragons are evil!" But the princess who had not seen the great fire but had seen the dragon, walked forward and said to the prince, "do not be afraid, the dragon can take us on the back of the wind to the place that awaits us." "But what if that place is evil?" stammered the prince.

"You have lived too long in fear," and with that the princess stepped up onto the leg of the dragon and onto its back. When he saw the princess looking so unafraid the prince stepped up behind her and then the mighty dragon lifted its scaly back and with one graceful beat of its wings lifted the prince and princess up over the forest and flew with them back to the kingdom of the prince.

The dragon set them down at last on a high hill overlooking the princes kingdom and the prince and princess walked home together hand in hand. When the prince, who had been away for a year and a day, returned home there was great rejoicing. All the people loved him and when they saw that he had brought with him a beautiful princess who would be his bride they were delighted and there was great feasting and celebrating for many days. At last the prince and princess made arrangements for their wedding and everyone was very excited. The old king, who loved his son dearly, took the young princess to his heart at once and all was well in the kingdom.

On the day of the hand-fasting the sun shone and the flags and banners made the castle look gay and festive. There was much excitement and activity as people prepared for a long and happy celebration. The prince and princess looked radiant as they walked hand in hand amongst the people. Suddenly the princess gave a start and clutched the prince's hand. "What is it?" asked the prince. "It is the old woman. I would know her anywhere," said the princess. The prince was very angry and shouted at the old woman. "How dare you come here on this important day, you who locked the princess in the tower for so long. Be gone from my kingdom old woman!" But the old woman looked at the prince with eyes that seemed to smoulder like the heart of an ancient fire and said in a gentle voice, "I have come to wish the princess well and to give you both my wedding gift. Do not be afraid any more prince, for it was not I who kept the princess in her tower for so long."
"Who could it have been then?"
"That you will have to ask the princess, for the door to the tower was never locked."

At this the startled prince looked at the princess but the princess, realising that she had kept herself prisoner all these years laughed and said, "So this is our story. We were both locked in our own towers until the day we met and saved each other. Thank you old woman, was this the gift you came to give us?"
"Ah no," replied the old woman. "The gift I have for you is the language of the dragon. Look deep into your heart and you will hear it and you will always know the answer to anything your heart desires, but listen well and be careful what you truly ask for, for you will always get exactly that." And with these words the old woman vanished into the crowd and then it seemed that a great and mighty dragon lifted her massive body from the hill and flew away into the heart of the sun.

With thanks to Naomi Mantin, Peter Morris, Maureen Amelia Brodie, Alexander Mackenzie and Ruth Mantin.

THINGS TO DO

Craft Ideas

Clearing Out

There are lots of things that can make clearing out a pleasant task. It is good to throw away, pass things on to others, or transform old things that are no longer useful.

Here are some ideas -
* have a patchwork party
* have a rag rug party
* have a craft party
* make beads out of paper to make jewellery or curtains
* recycle old sheets of paper to make new handmade paper
* make musical instruments from old tins and boxes or other items
* take things to a charity shop
* transform things to use as presents for Yule
* recycle rubbish
* have a bonfire and use it to let go of any unwanted thoughts, ideas or experiences that you want to let go of with the rubbish you cannot recycle

Recording Memories

There are many ways to do this. Writing a diary together, trying to remember what you did over the year is one way. If you have kept a diary of the year you will be able to read it and remember many happy times.

You could make a collage from lots of different photographs. You could mount them on corrugated cardboard cut from the side of a large box. One year we framed the card with dried leaves. You could find an old picture frame, as large as possible, and put your photographs in there. If you haven't got the wall space to put these up you might prefer to make a scrapbook and add things that have been collected such as tickets, programmes and photographs. The pages can be decorated in lots of different ways – for example, potato or block prints, coloured paper, painted patterns, or glitter.

Patchwork Party

The early history of patchwork is lost in time but there can be no doubt that it is as ancient as other kinds of needlework, which, because of their simplicity and economy, were of peasant origin. The term patchwork has been associated, in a general way, with needlework in which fragments of cloth are joined edge to edge by stitching or else applied as a decoration to the surface of a background material.

A characteristic of the American background to the work in its early days was the "Quilting Bee" - a party which was given when patchwork was done and friends and neighbours were invited to take part in the final work - when the quilt was put onto a frame and the quilting patterns stitched.

If you are having a party try to invite someone who enjoys patchwork to join you so that they can give guidance to those who need help. For hand sewing and particularly for patterns using diamonds and small patches, closely woven cottons are easiest to handle and give the best results. Heavier fabrics are suitable for larger pieces and machine sewing. Combining lightweight and heavier fabrics is difficult but can give dramatic and creative results.

Choose patterned material carefully. Large prints can over-dominate while small ones tend to merge into each other unless contrasted with plain fabrics.

You may like to start with a small item each, such as cushions or wall hangings, alternatively you may want to make one larger item together. Patches can be sewn by hand or machine. If you are working in a group it will be easier to work by hand. There are many excellent books on patchwork but here is a hand sewing method.

You will need
- a sharp sewing needle
- selection of material
- stiff paper (glossy magazine paper is ideal for weight)
- card (for template)
- sharp scissors (for material)
- scissors (for paper)
- tape

First cut out your templates (see below). Once you have chosen a design you will know what shapes you will need.

These must be made accurately because they are the patterns from which each shape is cut out. An error in size, however slight, will compound to several centimetres over an entire piece of work. For hand sewing with papers you will need three templates: one made 6mm (¼") bigger on all sides (used for cutting the fabric) make these from your card; the second made to the exact size of the finished patch (used for backing papers) make these from the magazine paper, and the third is a 'window' template if you are using patterned fabric, the same size as the first template.

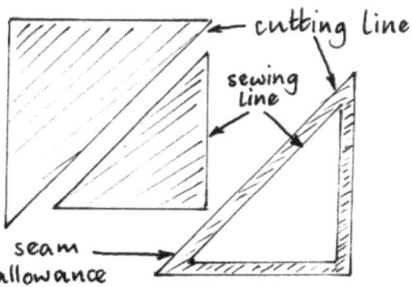

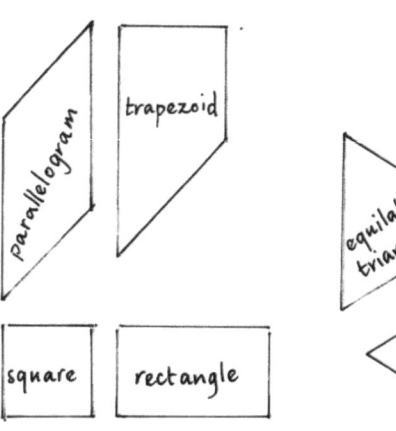

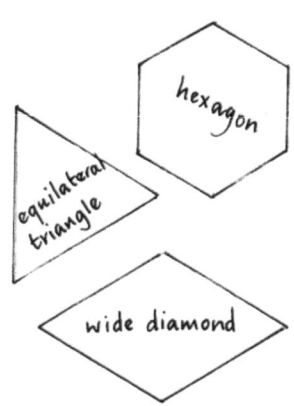

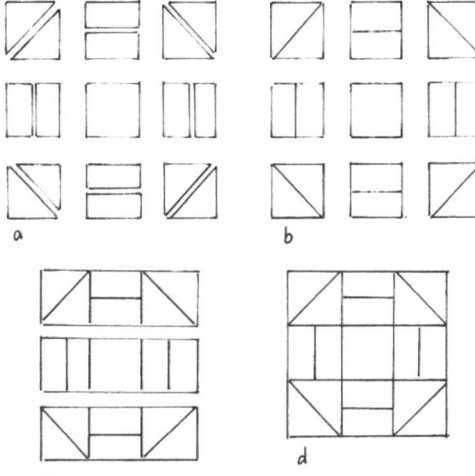

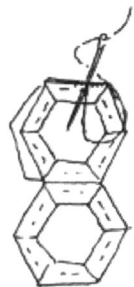

Lay your shapes out to see what they will look like. Use straight seams and avoid sewing into corners. It is easier to join the smallest pieces into progressively bigger units until the patchwork is complete. In the illustration the pieces are laid out and then the smallest pieces are sewn together. These are joined into rows and the rows then sewn together.

Use the bigger template and cut out your patches. When placing the template on the material, align the sides with the straight or cross grain where possible, avoiding the bias of the material which has the most stretch.
Lay your patch right side down and pin a paper template to the centre. Fold the material edge over and secure with tape.

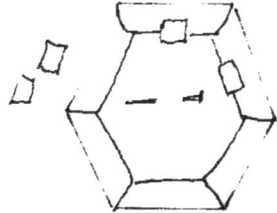

Tack all around the patch and carefully remove tape. Press the material folds – this makes sewing the patches much easier.
Individual patches are first joined with tiny overcastting stitches. Next the patches are joined into rows, with overcastting stitches. (Hexagons can be joined into rows or formed into rosettes.)

When all the patches are added and the paper removed, press the patchwork. Use a cloth to prevent glazing and iron on the back and then the top. After ironing you may wish to back your work with a single piece of cloth and add a border to edge the patchwork neatly. Additional decoration can be added in the form of embroidery stitches along existing seams, embroidered motifs or appliqué.

Appliqué

The word appliqué comes from the French verb meaning 'to apply', and refers to the technique of fixing shaped pieces of cloth onto a background fabric. The more of these I do, the more experimental I have become with the materials I have used. I now collect sweet papers, plastic, bark, net, gauze, feathers and many other things that might one day be used. I also collect boxes, which we decorate and use to store all our materials!
Often the simpler the design the more successful the appliqué will be. Shapes and patterns can be drawn directly onto fabric or cut freely with scissors. Again there are lots of excellent books, which will give you detailed instructions on this technique but here is a very simple version.

Choose a background colour and create a border of a different colour (or several). Sew the background to the border. Work from the background to the foreground. Sew the main objects onto the background using simple running stitch, tucking a hem under as you go.

Here are some hens - often used in traditional designs, but any subjects will do.

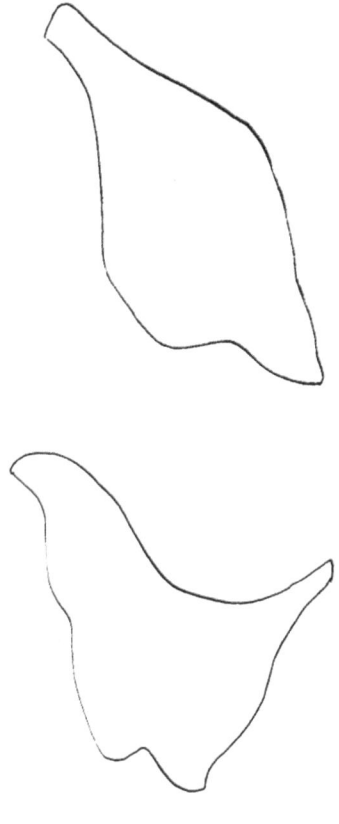

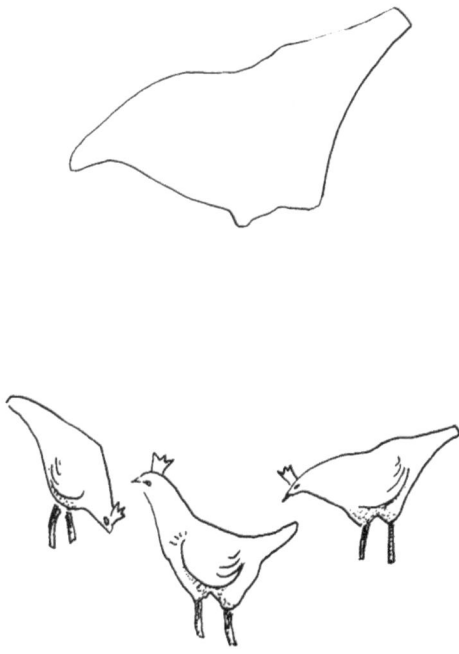

Rag Rug Party

During the long winter evenings families would gather in the kitchen to make mats. Old sacks, which were attached to a wooden frame, formed the base. Some members of the household would cut worn-out garments into strips while others hooked or prodded the ribbons of cloth through the hessian.

You may like to invite friends round to make a rag rug together or each to make individual items such as a small hanging.

For rag rugs you will need
- material in various colours (you can also use plastic carrier bags and any material that doesn't fray too much)
- Hessian or clean sack cut to size and hemmed
- rug hook or large crochet hook
- chinagraph pencil or wax crayon to mark design
- quilting frame if possible

Cut rags into long strips about 1.5cm (½") wide. Roll into balls if making a large rug. If you are working without a frame, work from the centre out, in order to maintain an even tension and prevent the base from being misshapen. If working with a frame, work from side to side and top to bottom. Work with the right side of the rug facing up.

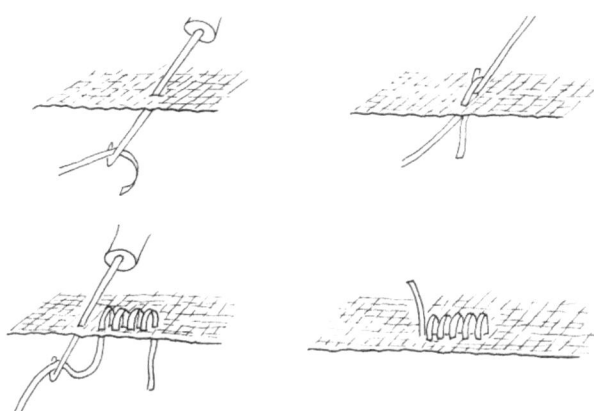

Hold a length of the fabric strip on the underside of the hessian with one end just under the starting point. Push the hook down through the cloth at a slight angle, catch the end of the strip and pull it through to the other side. Make the next hole as close as possible to the first, and bring up a small amount of the strip, forming a loop about 1.5cm(½") deep. Continue to the end of the strip, bringing it up to the surface to finish.

Trim the end level with the loops. Start a new strip in the hole where the previous strip ended.

Craft Party

This is a good way to spend time with your friends. I ask each person to bring something to nibble or eat/drink if we are meeting at an eating time of day. Depending on whether your friends are craft orientated or not, ask them to bring something they are making or you can have lots of things ready. I have invited people round and given them a basket full of dried leaves to make things from or a craft book and material, such as fir cones, tissue paper and cotton, and we have all had a lovely time making whatever we felt like. This is particularly good in the time running up to Yule when we are having fun making presents for each other. We have also made cards in this way.

Paper Beads

Paper beads always reminds me of Ronnie who made a beautiful bead curtain for her doorway out of magazine pictures inlaid with love letters. She told me that whenever she walked through the curtain she felt the warmth of the contents of the letters. Ronnie varnished her beads once they were dry.

You will need
- paper (magazine pictures, paintings, marbled paper, sweet papers, foil etc. and stick these inside the coloured paper.
- PVA or equivalent
- scissors
- knitting needle or cocktail stick

You can use as many layers for each bead as you like, just experiment so that you get the thickness you want.

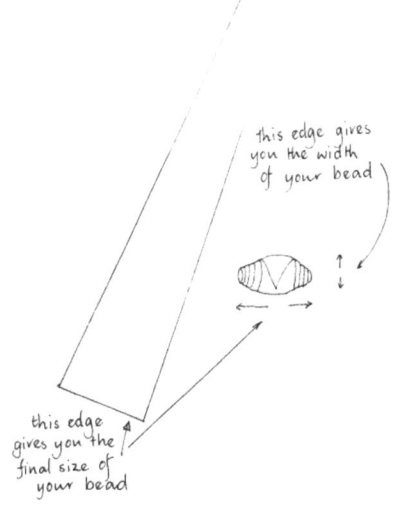

this edge gives you the width of your bead

this edge gives you the final size of your bead

Cut an isosceles triangle from your chosen paper about 25cm(10") long with a base about 3cm(1") or how ever long you want your finished bead to be and cover one side with glue.

Leave a small area at the wide end. If you are using more than one layer glue these together first.

Using a knitting needle or cocktail stick, starting at the wide end, roll the paper carefully around the needle until you get to the point, (this is why you should not put glue right up to the end of the paper). You will end up with a bead shape.

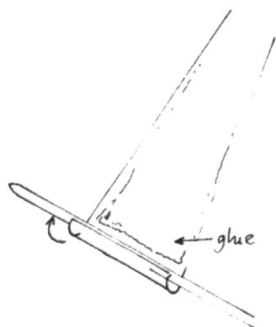

Leave to dry and then thread the beads together and use for jewellery, light pulls, hangings as the mood takes you.

Hand Made Paper

You will need
- paper - recycled paper makes it easier and computer print-out paper is particularly suitable. Newspaper should not be used as it soon discolours and glossy magazines are also unsuitable.
- liquidizer
- bucket
- rectangular washing-up bowl,
- a thin-bladed palette knife
- a simple wooden frame smaller than the washing-up bowl (this could be a disused picture frame)
- a piece of net curtaining or muslin to stretch across the frame and a stapler or some drawing pins to attach it.

Soak the waste paper in a bucket of water until it is thoroughly softened. In the meantime prepare the frame by stretching the net curtain over it and stapling or pinning it in place; this prepared frame is called a mould.

When the paper pulp has reached the required consistency place a handful of it, about the size of an egg, into the liquidizer three-quarters full of water (cold or warm). Run the liquidizer for about 20 seconds then check that a homogeneous liquid has formed. If any bits of unliquidized paper remain liquidize for a further 10 seconds. Make about 6 liquidizer loads, putting 5 of them into the plastic washing-up bowl and keeping one aside to add to the bowl as the level of the pulp becomes depleted.

Wet the net surface of the mould by running a wet hand over it; this helps the pulp to drain. Dip the frame vertically into the pulp at the far end of the bowl and then slide it horizontally under the surface of the pulp. Draw it through the pulp and then lift it out of the pulp holding it horizontal. Give it a little shake and allow it to drain.

Lay the frame on a piece of newspaper to finish draining then, after about an hour, place it outdoors or somewhere warm indoors to dry, tilted at an angle so that it will dry more quickly. When dry peel it from the mould with a pallet knife. It is also possible to turn the wet pulp from the mould onto a kitchen cloth to dry. This way you can make several sheets adding a kitchen cloth in between each new sheet.

Decorative detail can be added with petals, tealeaves, small ferns, confetti, or small pieces of coloured paper. Add these to the bowl of pulp and pick up at random.

Papier-Mâché

There are several ways of making papier-mâché.

Method One - (Bowl from Strips)

You will need
- paper torn into small strips (about 8 cm (3") x 1cm (½") or bigger if the item you are making is large)
- PVA or wall paper paste or equivalent glue mixed with equal quantity of water
- paint or glue brush
- petroleum jelly
- bowl or other simple object you want to recreate
- paints to decorate
- scissors

Coat the inside of the bowl with petroleum jelly. Paint each strip of paper with glue and cover the inside of the bowl with about five layers of the paper. Allow an overlap of about 2.5cm (1").

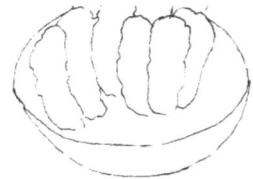

Leave to dry in a warm place for about 48 hours. Gently prise the paper bowl from its mould (you may need a knife) and leave it upside down to dry for a few hours.
Trim the ragged edge and add a layer of paper strips to neaten. Leave to dry.

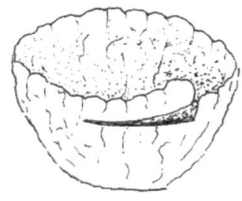

Paint or decorate the finished bowl. Varnish if required.
I have used tissue paper for this, which gives a finer, slightly translucent result. I have also added things like feathers in the last layer when using translucent paper.

Method Two - (Cut out Shapes)

You will need
- an item you have made out of corrugated cardboard (little shelves, a box, a picture frame, a heart etc.)
- paper tape (brown tape, paper on one side and glued on the other, usually available from art shops)
- a saucer of water to wet the tape
- paint to decorate

Once you have made your basic shape from cardboard, tear small strips of the tape, wet it in the water and stick on to your shape until it is completely covered and the result you want.

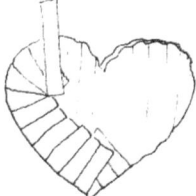

Paint or collage with coloured or patterned paper from magazines or old wrapping paper to decorate the finished item. Varnish if required.

Paper dipped in glue, as in method 1, can also be used on a cardboard base.

Method Three - (Puppet Head)

You will need
- very small pieces of news paper
- wall paper paste
- an old bucket
- hot water (hand hot)

Add the paste to the hot water (following instructions on the packet) and then add the strips of newspaper. Stir the mix as you add paper until you have the mixture very thick and difficult to stir.

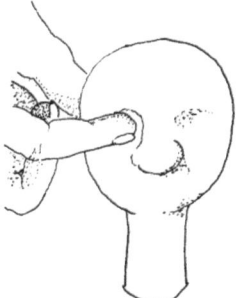

Allow this mixture to cool and take out a hand sized amount to mould, like clay, into the basic shape for the puppet head. Leave

enough of a neck to add a body made out of material.

Push your finger or a stick up inside the head to make the finger hole and leave the head to dry. Paint the face and add hair.

Sparkling Stars.

For each star you need
- 10 twigs about 15cm (6") long (take from fallen or coppiced branches)
- Some brightly coloured cotton thread
- Some glitter
- Glue

Decorate each twig by binding the thread around each one and adding glitter.

Use the cotton to tie four twigs together at each point of the star and then take two twigs to each of the points either side. Add any more decoration you like and then hang them up.

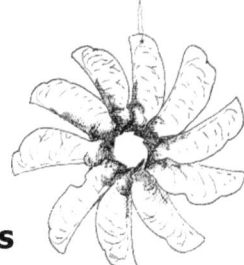

Wing Seed Flowers

This is an idea that Rae showed me one year.

You will need
- wing seeds like ash or sycamore
- card (optional)
- PVA glue or equivalent
- scissors

Ash keys

Collect a pile of wing seeds. Take the seeds out of the middle before they get dry and then arrange them in the shape of a flower - either glue them to each other or cut out a small circle from card and peg them to that. These can be hung on their own or used to make greeting cards.

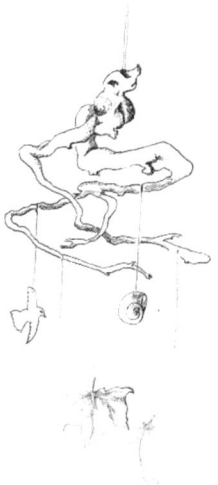

Mobiles

Anything can be hung to make a mobile. At this time of year it is easy to collect dried leaves, pinecones, bits of bark, feathers etc. and hang them from twigs. One year we found some beautiful twisted dried heather and used this as the base. Adding sequins and glitter can make the hanging catch the light but some people prefer to reflect the natural colours and shades of the season. A mobile can be a lovely way of recording your day / adventure / holiday / season / year.

Oak Rings

This is an idea I got from Jacqueline. Whenever I go to her house I am inspired by something she has been making. These can be used as wreaths to hang on the wall or for table decorations with a candle in the middle.

You will need
- thick card cut into a ring about the width of the oak leaves.
- dried fallen oak leaves
- glue
- metallic paint (optional)

Put glue onto the card ring and leave to go tacky.

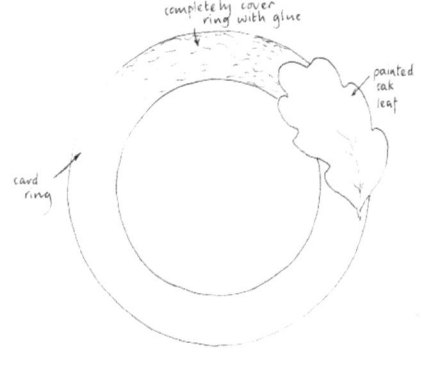

completely cover ring with glue

painted oak leaf

card ring

If you want to paint your oak leaves do so before sticking them to the ring. I have used gold mostly but I have also added different metallic colours to good effect. When the glue is ready stick the oak leaves around the ring and leave to dry. If you are hanging the ring up, you will need to add a little loop of wire to the ring before sticking on the leaves. It is also possible to use dried ivy leaves. Dry them by hanging them up or press them if you want a flatter effect.

Jack-O-Lanterns

Perhaps the most famous icon of Samhaine. Various authorities attribute it to either Scottish or Irish origin. However, it seems clear that it was used as a lantern by people who travelled the road on Halloween, the scary face to frighten away spirits or faeries that might otherwise lead one astray.

I remember how we used to make these out of turnips when I was young. Once you have cleared out all the rubbish and cleaned the house you can start to make the lanterns to welcome the ancestors or to guide your way home. These can be made from turnips, swedes, pumpkins, or any other large root vegetable.

Cut a slice about 5cm (2") from the top of the vegetable to make a lid. I usually cut a spiky line, as it is easier to replace after I have taken the lid off. Scrape out the flesh from the middle using an old spoon, leaving about 1.5cm (½") thickness of wall, and set aside to use in a vegetable stew or soup.

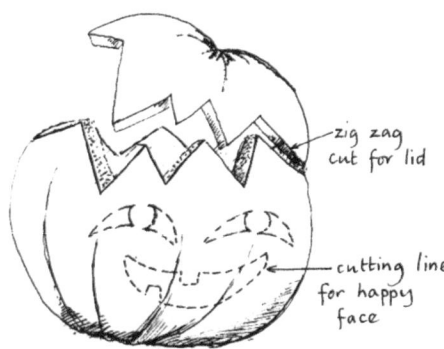

zig zag cut for lid

cutting line for happy face

Then cut or scrape a face or pattern out of the skin. There are two ways of doing this. Either cut right through the skin and flesh so that the light can shine through the hole or, alternatively cut the skin and some of the flesh away so that the light shines through a thin layer of flesh. A smiling face will welcome in the ancestors and let the neighbours know that you have been having fun!

Add a night light in the middle and then you can put your lanterns in the nature corner or hang in a window.

If you are going to stand it up you may need to cut a piece off the base to provide a flat surface. If you are hanging it up make sure you have a long enough length of string that won't get burned. If the lid is likely to burn cut a small hole above where the flame will be.

Paper Apple Chain

This apple chain can symbolise the Isle of Apples – Avalon.

You will need
- coloured paper
- scissors
- tape

Cut a strip of the coloured paper to the size you want your apples (I make them about 10cm (4") square. Concertina-fold the strip into sections the same width as the strip of paper so that you end with a folded square (in my case 10cm x 10cm (4" x 4"). If the end result is too thick you won't be able to cut it.

Draw the shape of an apple on the top square of the paper, with the sides of the apple touching the folded edges of the paper. Cut this shape out through all the layers of paper, leaving an uncut section of fold on each side.

Open the paper to see your apple chain. Add another chain of apples if you want a longer chain.

Write the names of anyone you wish to remember on each apple and hang across your altar in a special room. Imagine that on the shining isle they have eaten these apples and become new.

Moving On

Once the festival is over the season continues. The evenings get darker and fires warm the house. It is a time to be quiet and meditate on the things that we have learned. Time to be still and reflect on all the good things that we have gained and received and shared with our family and friends as we wait for the sun to return. Samhaine can be a still time as we make the most of the darkness and calm. This time of year can be difficult for those who are affected by the lack of sun or who are without family and loved ones. It is a kindness to be aware of those in our community who may need company or attention in some way.

November is our time for getting together and making little handmade presents for Yule and telling stories around the fire and for making our mincemeat ready for delicious mince pies or mincemeat flapjacks. We sometimes give jars of it away as presents.

Mincemeat

500g/1 lb cooking apples peeled
   and grated
125g/4ozs vegetable suet
250g/8ozs apricots chopped
900g/2 lbs mixed sultanas raisins
   and currents
50g/2ozs chopped or flaked
   almonds
50g/2ozs ground almonds
4 teaspoons mixed spice
1 teaspoon nutmeg
6 tablespoons brandy
2 oranges, juice and rind
1 lemon, juice and rind
375g/12ozs dark brown sugar

Mix all the above together and then cover it and leave to stand for 12 hours. Stir the mixture and bake in an oven for 3 hours on the lowest setting.

When it has finished cooking leave to cool slightly and put into jars covering the top of the mincemeat in each one with a dash of brandy.

This year I had to make sugar free mincemeat with no orange or lemon so I substituted the fruits with lime and grapefruit and used concentrated apple juice instead of sugar.

Flapjacks

125g/4ozs butter
75g/3ozs light brown sugar
75g/3ozs golden syrup or honey
1 large tablespoon mincemeat
250g/8ozs oats

Melt the butter and sugar together being careful not to boil. Remove from the heat and add the syrup, mincemeat and oats. Mix together and place in a shallow baking tin. Bake in a medium oven Gas mark 5 375F/190C for about 30 minutes.

Leave to cool slightly in the tin and then cut into fingers. If you like you can drizzle icing sugar over the top when completely cool.

Wheat free Pastry

This recipe was a mixture of trial and error and an idea from Sarah.

300/10ozs wheat free flour (I use a mixture
    of white rice, potato and tapioca flour)
 50g/2ozs ground almonds
 250g/8ozs butter
2 eggs

Mix the flours and almonds together into a mixing bowl. Add the butter and mix until they resemble breadcrumbs. Add the eggs until the dough begins to stick together. (Experiment with quantities until you get it how you like it.)

Orange Pastry

This is a recipe given to me by my cousin Penny. She likes to try out different ideas for cooking without wheat as her husband has several allergies. This one I particularly like for mince pies.

 375g/12ozs wheat free flour
 50g/2ozs icing sugar
 250g/8ozs butter
 finely grated rind and juice of 1 orange

Sift the flours and sugar together into a mixing bowl. Add the butter and mix until they resemble breadcrumbs. Add the orange rind and then stir in the orange juice until the dough begins to stick together. Refrigerate before using.

Wheat free Brownies

We love this recipe as it was one of the first successful wheat free ones we tried. I used the brownies in my daughter's school lunch box quite often as a treat.

 150g/6ozs butter
 125g/4ozs icing sugar
 250g/8ozs raw brown caster sugar
 2 eggs, beaten
 250g/8ozs wheat free flour
 125g/4ozs hazel nuts, chopped

Grease a shallow 8" square tin Melt the butter and chocolate together and then add the sugar. Mix in the eggs, the flour and a pinch of salt. Add the chopped nuts.
Cook on Gas mark 4/350F/180C for 30 – 45 minutes.

Clove and Orange Candles

You will need
    - small oranges
    - night-lights
    - pen
    - whole cloves
    - a small sharp knife
    - small spoon

To make one candle, first of all make sure your orange will stand up on its own. If not, cut a small strip from the bottom.

Place the night light on top of the orange and draw round it with the pen.

Following the pen circle cut out a hole and then scoop out the inside of the orange until you have enough space to put your night-light in.
Put the cloves around the edge of the night-light to finish it off.

Song for Samhaine
Gently Now The Earth

A gentle round that reflects the season.
Can be sung in two parts.

H.Royall

Gently now the earth prepares to sleep, So cold the

winds Demeter weeps, Fly away, the winter soon will be

here, Autumn time, leaves fall, leaves fall.

Winter Solstice
Time for Presents

WINTER SOLSTICE
(21st or 22nd December)

As the nights grow longer and the air colder the atmosphere in our homes changes, we are less inclined to go out and we try to keep ourselves cosy with light, heat and warm, comforting food. The birth of a child has always been celebrated at this time of year, whether it was the return of the sun, the Star Child of Promise, Jesus, Dionysus, Attis, Mithras, all have been welcomed, celebrated and delighted in, giving us a real reason to rejoice.

Perhaps in earlier times, people would have been less sure than we are today that the sun would return, that the days would begin to get longer and the winter not cover the world with its frozen mantle. They might have put their effort into chants and spells to call back the sun until, by a few minutes a day, the nights would begin to shorten and the people could rejoice and the best of the stored foods be brought out, bonfires lit on the hilltops, decorations of greenery festoon the homes and gifts for the children be given and received. There were round dances, called 'carols', special songs and wild fragrance of holly, ivy and mistletoe to enrich this darker time. We love the heady smell of pine whenever we have a green tree in the house at this time of year.

Now make you merry, gentlemen,
Let nothing you dismay,
Cold winter now is set to flight
The sun returns today,
To keep us all from dark and cold
He has not gone away,

O, tidings of comfort and joy,
comfort and joy,
O, tidings of comfort and joy!

Now make you merry, ladies,
The dark is on the run,
For blessed light does now return
And so begins our fun,
Lets drink a cup of friendship here,
And then another one!

O, tidings …

Now make you merry, children,
A star returns this night,
For the dear Child of Promise
Gives us his gentle light,
To keep us all from dark and cold
There're presents warm and bright,

O, tidings …

Now to the Sun sing praises,
All you within this place,
And like a loving company
Each other now embrace,
The happy time of longer days
Is drawing on apace,

O, tidings …

With thanks to Norman Isles

In Starhawk's book 'The Spiral Dance' she tells of the tradition to meet at the beach just before sunset on the eve of Winter Solstice. You can imagine the thrill of the wonderful atmosphere that must be arise as they build a fire and chant to gather their courage before jumping into a chilled ocean for cleansing. She tells of the all night vigil that follows, which leads to the meeting at dawn and the climb to the city's hills and the chanting and drumming until the sun comes up (or until the mist grows light). The children have their own ritual in which they decorate round cookies to represent the sun. They receive gifts, tell stories and each child receives a red floating candle that they can light and let burn until morning.

Let us be inspired at this time of year to rejoice at the return of the sun and maybe our rejoicing will become our rituals that we look forward to when all else is dark. Winter Solstice is the time to gather together and celebrate; to be joyful and give thanks for all that is to come. This is the time to give and receive presents, to cook wonderful meals from the generous harvest and to be witness to the miracle of birth, new life and the constant turning of the seasonal cycle.

Goddess for Winter Solstice

Hestia

Hestia sits by the fireside at the heart of the home. Her large, comfortable body exudes the calm and peace that brings people together in community. As she presides over the cooking of bread and the preparation of the family meal she gives her blessing to all domestic happiness.

Choose a place in your home that represents its heart and place a sacred object there that represents Hestia. We have a beautiful, hand-crafted pottery vase, in the shape of a seated woman. You could use a candle or lantern to represent the fire or something red or gold. Her symbol is a kettle.

One tradition, sacred to Hestia, is that when a family moves home they take a flame from their old home with them. Traditionally, the fire should always be kept burning and, if it goes out, should be lit again from fire kindled from friction or from the magnified heat of the sun. Nowadays many homes do not have an open fire and do not keep candles burning. When my daughter moved I took her a candle which I had burned in my home, near my symbol of Hestia. We re-lit it as a symbolic welcome to the house and a blessing on the heart of her new home.

A CHRISTMAS CAROL
(THE SECOND OF THE THREE SPIRITS)

Charles Dickens

It was his own room. There was no doubt about that. But it had gone through a surprising transformation. The walls and ceiling were so hung with living green that it looked a perfect grove, from every part of which, bright gleaming berries glistened. The crisp leaves of holly, mistletoe and ivy reflected back the light, as if so many little mirrors had been scattered there; and such a mighty blaze went roaring up the chimney, as that dull petrification of a hearth had never known in Scrooge's time, or Marley's, or for many and many a winter season gone. Heaped up on the floor, to form a kind of throne, were turkeys, geese, game poultry, brawn, great joints of meat, sucking-pigs, long wreaths of sausages, mince-pies, plum-puddings, barrels of oysters, red-hot chestnuts, cherry-cheeked apples, juicy oranges, luscious pears, immense twelfth-cakes, and seething bowls of punch, which made the chamber dim with their delicious steam. In easy state upon this couch, there sat a jolly Giant, glorious to see; who bore a glowing torch, in shape not unlike Plenty's horn, and held it up, high up, to shed its light on Scrooge, as he came peeping round the door.

'Come in!' exclaimed the ghost. 'Come in and know me better, man!'

Scrooge entered timidly, and hung his head before this spirit. He was not the dogged Scrooge he had been; and though the Spirit's eyes were clear and kind, he did not like to meet them.

'I am the Ghost of Christmas Present,' said the Spirit. 'Look upon me!'

Scrooge reverently did so. It was clothed in one simple deep green robe, or mantle, bordered with white fur. This garment hung so loosely on the figure that its capacious breast was bare, as if disdaining to be warded or concealed by any artifice. Its feet, observable beneath the ample folds of the garment, were also bare; and on its head it wore no other covering than a holly wreath, set here and there with shining icicles. Its dark brown curls were long and free: free as its genial face, its sparkling eye, its open hand, its cheery voice, its unconstrained demeanour, and its joyful air. Girded round its middle was an antique scabbard; but no sword was in it, and the ancient sheath was eaten up with rust.

THINGS TO DO

Time for Presents

When my daughter was younger we collected books that reflected the season and put them in a decorated box, and read them together. There were certain books that we really looked forward to reading again each year especially the winter books. Now she is older we look forward to hearing certain tapes and CDs that are in season while we sit and make things or cook. We also love putting on a story tape while we work.

On the first day of December we start our count down to Winter Solstice when the sun will return.

We have made a little velvet bag for each member of the family and extra in case we have guests. Each morning we give each other a little present in the bag.

The presents would be very simple and preferably home made. We make things like pressed leaves, feathers with tiny beads round the stem, or simple jewellery, usually something that we can hang on a branch on our table display. The only requirement being that it can fit into the bag! We also have a beautiful branch, painted and covered with glitter that stands on our nature table and a star shaped basket filled with little stars that we made one year. Each morning we take a star out of the basket and hang it on the branch. On the 21st December the last thing we take out of the basket is a little paper sun.

We don't allow ourselves to sing carols or eat mince pies until the first day of December so we really look forward to that date and the house takes on a very festive feel.

On the 21st of December we give each other presents, one main one usually, and from then on we seem to be giving and receiving presents until the end of the month. We have a beautiful glass sun, which we hang up in place of the moon, that hangs over our nature corner and we put a tree in the front room, which we decorate. We have had mixed feelings about fir trees coming into the house each year. I am not sure that we wish to support the industry that grows the trees that are not good for the earth, only to be cut down and left to die. We have experimented with potted trees that we replant (again this is not good for the earth as they can get very big and some companies boil the roots so that they will die and a new tree will have to be purchased the following year). We have also tried artificial trees and no tree. Our most successful tree was a fallen branch that we painted white and decorated with clear glass ornaments. It looked very beautiful as if it was covered with frost and has inspired us to collect clear glass ornaments each year. This year I bought a beautiful lollipop shaped bay tree and decorated that with lights and delicate ornaments. However there are those traditionalists who suggest that such a tree should be cut down rather than purchased, and should be disposed of by burning, the proper way to dispatch any sacred object.

Once, the Yule log was the centre of the celebration. It was lit on the eve of the solstice (it should light on the first try) and had to be kept burning for twelve hours, for good luck. Later, the Yule log was replaced by the Yule tree but, instead of burning it, burning candles were placed on it.

Our tree goes up in the morning ready for our party in the evening. We also go for a walk and collect greenery and then come home and decorate the house with holly and ivy and hang a large bunch of mistletoe in the front room. The mistletoe will stay up until next December 21st of the following year when it will be replaced with the new green branch. One year I sprayed the old branch gold at the beginning of December.

As the rest of my family celebrated Christmas and other friends had a special visit from Father Christmas, we did the same for a while, but when my daughter was older we talked about the Lord of Winter, represented by the holly tree, who comes with his promise to protect us through the dark winter months.

Dressed in green with a wreath of holly around his head, possibly the Green Man or Herne the Hunter, he joins in our celebrations bidding us be mindful of those who need comfort and joy at this dark time. (Later this green Lord changed his coat for a red one for a Coca-Cola advert and turned into a jolly fat man with no particular significance other than familiarity.) On the 21st we go shopping and fill a basket with food. This we take to someone who needs it. We try to leave it on their doorstep and not get caught but that is not always possible. We are not always aware of people in our community who might need help at this time of year, but when we know and we will be preparing to give the Yuletide basket to someone, it can help us to be mindful.

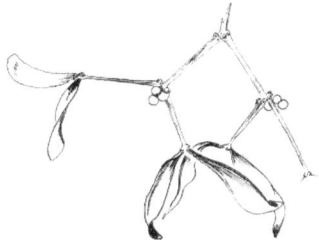

I have always only invited women friends to my Winter Solstice celebration. This is my particular decision and it has worked very well so far. We follow certain traditions that have grown over the years. We each bring a small present for everyone who comes and take it in turn to give them out. This can take a long time and is most enjoyable. The presents are small and simple and beautifully wrapped. While we are waiting for everyone to arrive we make a pile of the presents under the tree and a very attractive pile it is. By the time we have given and opened the presents it is time to eat. We always have a wonderful cheese board full of delicious cheeses and a bunch of grapes, savoury biscuits, a bowl of mixed dry roast vegetables that are like crisps but much tastier, and a hot chestnut and vegetable stew. We also have mulled wine and mulled apple juice. It is a wonderful feast. We share Tarot readings and listen to or join in some carol singing. We put fresh mistletoe up in place of the old and each person is given a small piece to take home.

Some ideas for things that can be bought for the bags or for Solstice presents are night-lights, small candles, candle holders, tree ornaments, brooches, earrings, sweets, photographs, cakes, lanterns and any small seasonal thing that doesn't cost much.

Craft Ideas

Dried Leaves

Collect different coloured and shaped leaves and press them between pages of a large book, like a telephone directory, or put them between pieces of clean paper and put several heavy books on top of them. When they are dry decorate them with glitter or gold and silver paint. One nice idea is to put very fine glitter just on the edges of the leaf to make it look as if it is covered in frost

Hanging Beads

Collect glass bead necklaces from car boot sales or second hand shops, or look through your old jewellery and see what you can find. Take the necklaces apart and make small hangings from the beads. These look lovely hung on windows or from lampshades. You can make a single row hanging or several rows together. It is also possible to add sequins or little star or angel shapes.

Paper Flowers

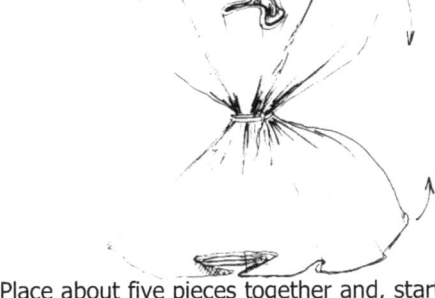

You will need
- crêpe paper
- scissors
- wire or cotton thread

Very simple carnations can be made from crêpe paper. Cut several oblongs of crêpe paper - the size will depend on what size you want your flower to turn out. You need to ensure that the paper is cut with the longest side going across the grain.

Place about five pieces together and, starting at the shortest edge, concertina the paper up until you get to the other end. Tie the centre with wire or cotton thread.

Separate the individual pieces of crêpe paper all along the longest edges until you have a pretty puffed up flower head.

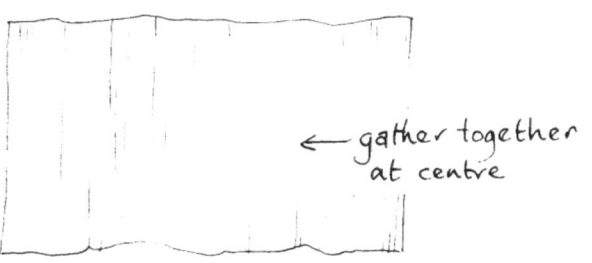

← gather together at centre

You can use one or several colours. It is also possible to make these into ball shapes to put in your green leaf arrangements or for garlands.

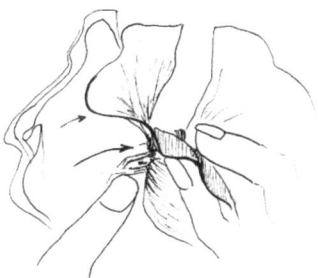

Pot Fairies

These are little things on sticks that can stand in potted plants or vases. They can be angels, reindeer, birds, fairies, insects, people, shapes, words or anything else you care to imagine.

I have described using stiff card here but you could also use natural things like acorn cups, beech masts, twigs, and sheep's wool. Dried daffodil petals make lovely fairy wings.

You will need
- stiff card
- colours (paint or crayon)
- glitter
- any other material to decorate
- scissors
- garden stick or barbecue skewer

Cut two of the same shape out of card. Add colour, glitter or decorate in any way you choose.

Stick them together either side of the stick. You may like to varnish it if you think water splashing on it will spoil it.

Cut Out Shapes

Any shape can be used, cut out of card or corrugated card (like you find on boxes) - star, heart, fish, angel etc.

You will need
- stiff card
- sequins and glitter
- paint
- cotton thread

Cut out your shape and decorate with sequins or glitter and add a little piece of cotton thread to hang it up with.

To make the shape padded, add narrow strips of brown paper tape (as in papier-mâché method two, page 34), leave to dry and decorate.

Finger Puppets

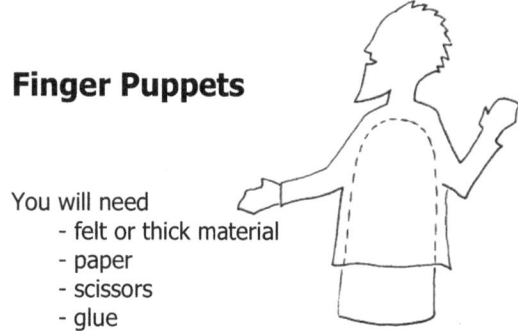

You will need
- felt or thick material
- paper
- scissors
- glue

Draw around your finger onto a piece of paper to work out what size you will need and cut the shape out of the paper.

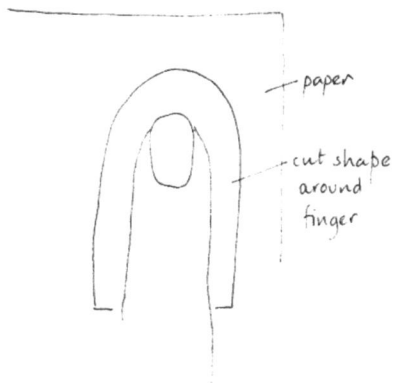

paper

cut shape around finger

Place the finger shape onto the material and cut a dome shape leaving enough room, about 1cm extra, for the finger and the hem. Sew or glue together.

Cut out the shape for your character and stick it on top of the dome shape.

Peppermint Creams

You will need

- 38g/1½ ozs cream cheese
- 125g/5ozs icing sugar
- a few drops of peppermint essence

Mix the cream cheese and icing sugar together until smooth. The mixture should be firm, so adjust if necessary.

Add the peppermint essence, one drop at a time (it is easy to put in too much, so test as you go!). You can leave the mixture white or add a very small amount of food colouring.

Roll out to about 0.5cm (¼") on a board lightly dusted with icing sugar and cut out little shapes or break off little pieces, roll into a ball and press into a disc. Leave to dry on sheets of greaseproof paper. Try not to eat them all before you give them away as presents!

One year we made little stars and lightly dusted them with icing sugar and arranged them in little baskets. The arms of the stars tended to break off so we will use a more rounded star shape next time.

Little Twig Stars

Use the same method for the sparkly stars on page 36, only make them smaller.

Willow Stars

You will need

- 120 cms (50") length thin strips of
  willow, soaked until pliable
- decorative thread (optional)

Soak the willow until it will bend easily without breaking.

Fold the strip in half. Bend into five equal lengths before working into position.

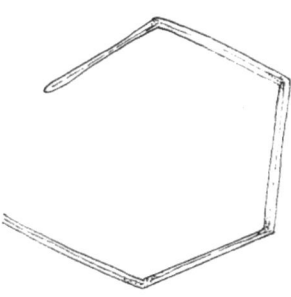

Twist the willow into the star shape and tuck the ends into the loop as in the diagram.
You may like to decorate the points by twisting decorative thread in and out of them. You could also use coloured wire or strips of paper.

Tissue Paper Stars

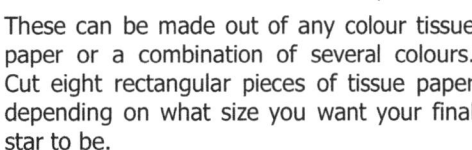

You will need
- tissue paper
- scissors
- light paper glue

These can be made out of any colour tissue paper or a combination of several colours. Cut eight rectangular pieces of tissue paper depending on what size you want your final star to be.
Fold the sheets lengthways and unfold them again.

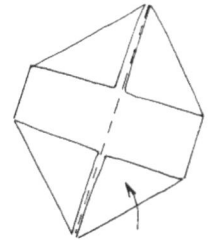

Fold the four corners in to the centre line so that a point is made above and below. You may want to stick the corners down with a bit of glue.

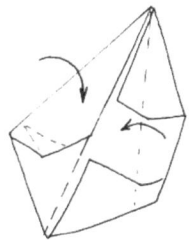 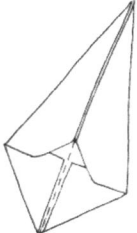

From the top point, fold the two sides once again to the centre line. This sharp point makes one of the points of the star; the wider lower points form the middle of the star.
Once all the eight points have been folded, stick the star carefully together.

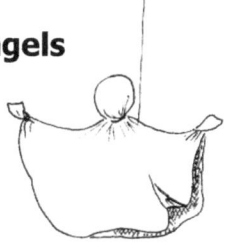

Tissue Paper Angels

You will need
- white or coloured tissue paper circles
- sheep's wool
- white cotton thread

Take a circle of paper. Roll up a little piece of teased sheep's wool into a ball and put it into the centre of the circle.

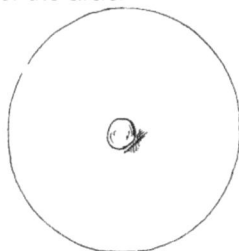

Fold the tissue paper over the sheep's wool so that the two edges meet, shape it and tie off the head with a white thread.

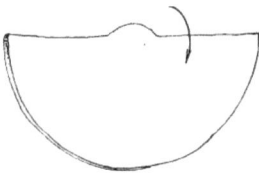

Twist the edges of the tissue paper at each end to form hands.

Attach a fine piece of cotton to the head to hang your angel up. One year my daughter made an angel mobile on a beautiful, twisted piece of ivy. I still have it hanging in my bedroom even though it is a little faded.

Willow Star Lanterns

You will need
- 5 x 55cms (21") willow strips
- 5 x 15cms (6") willow strips
- small jar
- masking tape
- garden wire
- wet strength tissue paper
- water based glue
- string
- stick

Make two stars by joining the long willow strips and securing with masking tape.

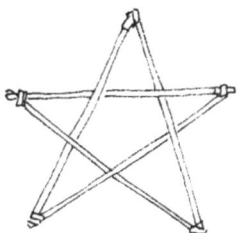

Again using masking tape join the two stars together by attaching the shorter willow strips to the pentacles formed by the centre of the stars as in the diagram.

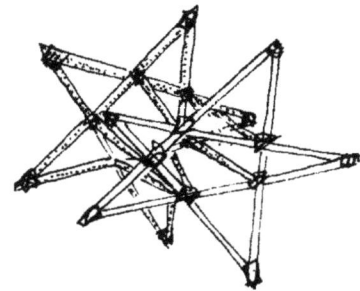

Make a loop of wire and secure it around the neck of the jar so that a short length is left over. Make another loop of wire and secure it around the neck of the jar so that a short length is left over on the opposite side.

Using the short lengths at each side attach the jar to the inside of the structure as in the diagram.

Put a night light in the jar.
Stick the ends of the two stars together as shown.

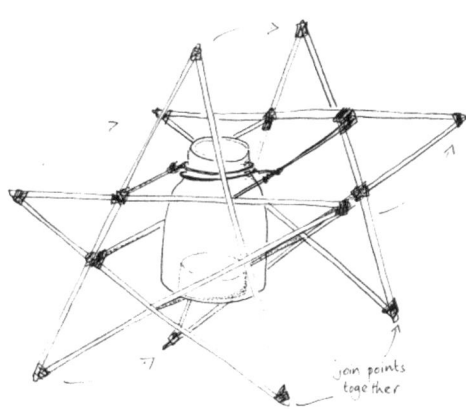

join points together

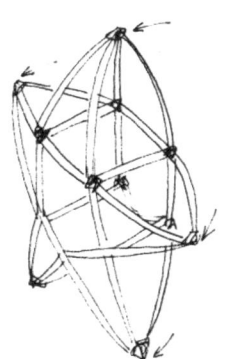

Cover the structure with wet strength tissue paper leaving a 'chimney' at the top of the star.
Attach the top point of the star to the stick using the string. Make sure it is long enough to be safe when the lantern is lit.

top left uncovered

Sand Lanterns

For this you will need to find or make a substantial white paper bag with a flat bottom. You may need to cut a bag down to a smaller size.

You will need
  - paper bags
  - needle
  - sand
  - night light

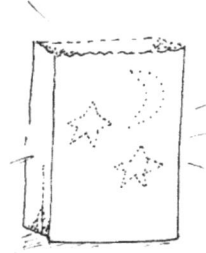

Make a pattern on the sides of the bag using a needle and pricking little holes. Be careful not to go below 3cm (1") from the bottom. Fill the bag with sand to about 3cm (1") and put a night-light in it.

Use less sand if the bag is smaller but make sure the bag will not catch fire with a candle in it.

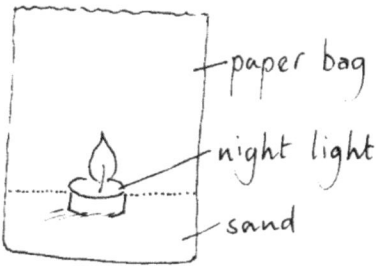

Tin Lanterns

Apart from paper, tin cans are probably the greatest throwaway items in any dustbin. Here is a lovely idea for using up an old tin can of any size.

You will need
- a clean tin can
- paper to design pattern
- pencil
- hammer
- nail punch or large nail for larger holes
- small nails for smaller holes
- an old screwdriver for long holes (optional)
- tin opener for drinks cans for triangular holes (optional)
- piece of wood or dowel large enough to fit neatly into the cans

There are two ways of preparing your can. Clean your can and remove the labels. If there are any sharp edges around the lip of the can use a hammer to flatten them and smooth the surface. Then either fill it with water and put it in the freezer until the water is frozen or put your piece of wood inside the can and then punch holes into the can.

If you want to work out a design first, cut a piece of paper to fit around your can. If you want a repeating pattern, open the paper to a flat surface and divide it into a number of sections of equal size.

Draw on your design. You can vary the shape of the holes by using different implements as your punching tools.

If you are following a design, wrap your design around the can and secure. Punch holes through the paper. If you want to use the design again, make very light indents in the can and remove the paper design before punching the holes.

Once you get the hang of it you can make some very intricate patterns but any pattern, however simple, looks good. If you want a handle make holes at each side of the can for string. Make sure the string is long enough so that it doesn't get too near the flame.

Shapes from Foil

Collect the foil tops from yoghurt or margarine tubs etc. They need to be plain foil with no writing on.

You will need
- foil
- scissors
- pieces of newspaper or thick card
- blunt pencil or pointed tool

Cut out a shape and put it onto several layers of newspaper or card. Using a bluntish pencil or a pointed tool and working from the wrong side make a pattern of little embossed dots and lines. Names and endearments can be written but remember to write in mirror fashion.

3D Stars

You will need
- thick card or paper
- pencil
- scissors
- ruler
- decoration if required

Cut out a star shape - five six or eight pointed - from thick paper (I have used embossed paper, handmade paper and card, so experiment and see what works best for you).

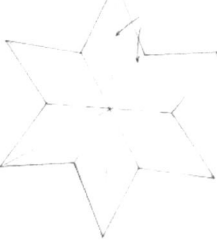

On the reverse of the star draw straight lines from the points to the centre of the star and from the centre to the indented corners.
If the paper is very thick, or you are using card, score before folding the long lines from the reverse side and the short lines from the right side.

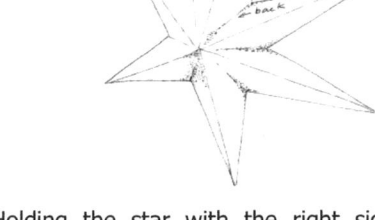

Holding the star with the right side away from you fold the points down along the centres of the long lines, and up along the shorter lines. Add decoration if needed.

Dragon Boats

You will need
- thick card
- scissors
- masking tape
- short, glass headed pins
- brightly coloured thread
- glue

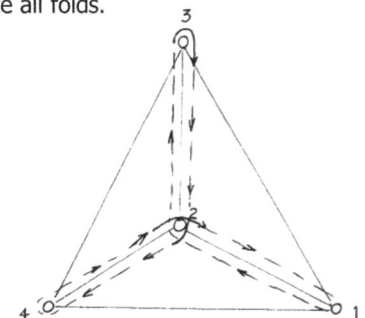

Cut a rectangle from a piece of card, the length should be three times the width. Score along the dotted lines as shown and fold the card into a hexahedron. Using masking tape reinforce all folds.

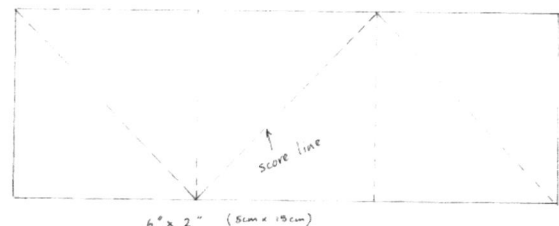

Place five glass headed pins (short if you can get them) on each of the points. Holding one side towards you (lowest point uppermost) number the pins 1 to 4 (you won't be able to see the fifth one).

Using brightly coloured thread take a length and secure the end with tape or glue and start to wind one side of the hexahedron - 1 .. 2 .. 3 .. 2 .. 4 .. 2 .. 1 .. 2 .. 3 .. 2 etc. changing colours as you please until the whole of the boat is covered, ending at the fifth pin head. Tuck the last thread in and glue if necessary.

Gingerbread House

Sometime in December a friend of mine always makes a gingerbread house with her children. We tried it one year and had a lot of fun. We decorated it with dried fruit and nuts and a small amount of icing sugar for the roof, dripping down like icicles. I have never found a good light recipe for gingerbread so I buy a kit. We eat the house on the 21st at the party.

Fruity Pudding

Makes 2 x 800g/1¾ lb puddings

50g/2ozs wholemeal flour
2.5ml/½ tsp mixed spice
1.25 ml /¼ tsp nutmeg
225g/8ozs currents
225g/8ozs sultanas
225g/8ozs raisins
175g/6ozs breadcrumbs
100g/4ozs suet
50g/2ozs ground or chopped almonds
    small cooking apple
225g/8ozs raw brown sugar
3 eggs
grated rind and juice of half orange
100ml/4fl ozs sherry

Thoroughly combine all the ingredients until evenly mixed. Grease 2 pudding basins and press the mixture into them. Cut 2 large circles of greaseproof paper - about 10cm(4") larger than the tops of the pudding basins - brush them with oil and make a pleat in each so that the pudding can expand. Place over the basins and secure with string. Top with a piece of kitchen foil. Steam for 6 hours. Reheat by steaming for a further one and a half hours.
If you are organised you can collect little silver charms through the year to put in your pudding.

Spiced Cranberry and Orange Sauce

75g/3ozs granulated sugar
150ml/¼ pint fresh orange juice
175g/6ozs fresh cranberries
½ teaspoon ground cinnamon
½ teaspoon ground nutmeg

Stir the sugar into the orange in a pan, add the cranberries and spices and stir. Bring to the boil and simmer for 5 minutes.

Ruthie's Spicy Cakes

One of the recipes my daughter made up has gradually evolved into these delicious little spicy cakes. She uses a small bun tray but any cake tray will do.

100g/4ozs butter
100g/4ozs sugar
2 eggs, beaten
50g/2ozs wheat free flour
50g/2ozs ground almonds
1 teaspoon ground mixed spice
½ teaspoon ground ginger
½ teaspoon ground cinnamon
½ teaspoon ground nutmeg
Small handful of currants

Grease 12 bun tins. Mix the butter and sugar together until light and fluffy. Beat in the eggs and then blend in the flour, almonds and spices. Add the currants and cook on Gas Mark 5/375F/190C for 15 minutes or until golden brown.

Song for Winter Solstice
Holly and Mistletoe

H.Royall

Hol - ly and mis - tle - toe here we go, here we go,

Hol - ly and mis - tle - toe, dance we round a gain.

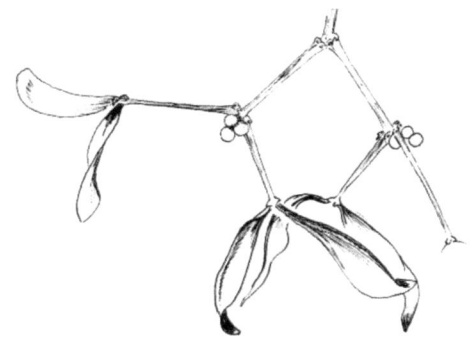

Imbolc
Welcoming the New

IMBOLC
(Pronounced Imelc)
(2nd February)

At Imbolc, the Goddess returns, and the Earth rejoices as the might of winter loosens its grip on the land. In many areas white snowdrops can be seen nodding their bright heads above the melting snow and the brightly coloured crocuses lift their heads as Persephone steps on the frozen earth again after her long work underground. Life awakens as new lambs are born in sheltered pastures and Mother Nature is renewed, as she becomes the Maiden of Spring.

The Celtic name for this celebration is 'Oimelc', literally 'ewes' milk', which would have been a vital part of the family's nourishment at this starved time of year. It is also known as The Feast of Brigit, Candlemas and Groundhog day. For thousands of years 40 days after the Winter Solstice has been a special festival sacred to women, and at this time we celebrate the festival of the White Goddess Brigid, a celebration involving the women of the household (men joining in later). Before the advent of the written calendar, people relied on nature's own calendar to show them when the Goddess had come back. In the northern hemisphere, spring arrives with the thaw. According to Paddy Slade in her book 'Natural Magic', in olden times farmers used to take their trousers off and sit on the ground at Imbolc to find out if it was warm enough to plough.

Together we have found different ways to celebrate the coming of spring and the thawing of the land. We made some beautiful white robes, my daughter's was silver like the glittering snow, and we lit a large white candle to put in the centre of the table at meal times. We have taken a bowl of snow and lit a candle in the middle allowing the snow around it to gradually melt to represent the thaw; a table full of snowdrops, crocus and other available flowers (we prefer to use potted rather than cut flowers where possible); a meal served in a cauldron or a cauldron of water in the centre of the table. At the mealtime we ask each person what commitment they are going to make to the coming year. We try not to prepare for this part and see what spontaneous ideas come up. It is good to have something to work on as the year unfolds and it is also very important to work on loving yourself enough to help yourself stay committed. (We make a point of not allowing anyone to use this as an excuse to criticize her or himself if they can't finish what they set out to achieve!) You may like to give out small candles to your friends and family to represent their hopes and wishes as spring gives us hope for the year, and, if you make candles, this is a good time of year to do so; they can then be blessed and, if you make enough, can last you for the whole year.

One of the nicest folk-customs still practiced in many countries is to place a lighted candle in every window of the house, beginning at sundown on Imbolc eve (February 1st), allowing them to continue burning until sunrise. Make sure they are safe and won't catch the curtains or tip over, as sadly, the number of house fires has risen due to more people using candles for decoration with little thought or respect for the power of fire. What a wonderful sight to see so many windows lit up on such a dreary night.

This is the time of year to look for new beginnings. Sometimes it is hard to believe that warmth and light will ever come again! Go for walks and feel the season turning and see who can be the one to get the first sightings of snowdrops. Make sure all your Winter Solstice decorations are put away before Brigit comes. This is the time of year for giving thanks for all that we have had and seeing what we can give away. Invite your friends round for a pot-luck dinner, take something to a charity shop, make some craft things to put in a present drawer, give to charity or make a commitment to sponsor someone or something, get involved in a community project or spring clean your house and learn from the disciplines of Feng Shui how to best use the energies in your home space.

Goddess for Imbolc

Rhiannon

Rhiannon rises out of the sea on a white mare. Her blue-green robe swirls around her like water and her long hair falls over her shoulders echoing the waves of her beloved sea. Rhiannon falls in love with each individual person she meets, thus teaching them what it is to be loved. She carries an apple of wisdom and gives each person a bite so that they will speak only truth and learn to live in bliss.

As spring moves into summer the people raise white poles in honour of her beautiful strong mare and tie ribbons around it and dance their May dances, rejoicing in their unions. Rhiannon is the Goddess of Love and the sacred union between two people. Her symbols are white birds, small white flowers, and apples.

AT THE CROSSROADS

Once at a crossroads, where the road going east and west met the road going north and south, there sat a naked teenager. People who passed her were very upset or embarrassed and wouldn't go near, especially other teenagers. Some called her names, some looked the other way and some threw clothes at her to put on but the girl just sat and ignored them.

One day a young, fashionable girl came up to her and said, "You must be cold sitting here with nothing on, take my jeans and put them on." The naked girl took the jeans and said, "But these are very heavy, why is that?" The fashionable girl replied, "Oh don't think it's easy always being up to date with the fashion. You must always be changing your clothes to make sure you are not seen wearing something that has gone out of the current fashion, and once you've been seen wearing something you can't wear it again. You must constantly be aware of what other people think of you and only be seen around with other people who are also in the fashion."
"I don't want these jeans, here take them back." But the young girl dropped them on the ground and continued to talk to the naked girl.

"Soon a very rich young teenager came along and saw the two girls sitting talking and he came to join them. You must be cold," he said and handed the naked girl his leather jacket. "This is heavy too," said the girl. "Of course it is," said the rich boy, "do you think it's easy being rich? I can have anything I want as long as I'm seen to show off my parent's wealth. I never get to make my own mind up about real issues and I have to be seen in all the right places.
My clothes say more about what I have than who I am." The naked girl said, "I don't want it, take it back," but the boy dropped the jacket with the jeans and soon the fashionable girl and boy were discussing who had the harder life.
A young, intelligent, hardworking girl heard the argument and saw the naked girl. "Take my dress," she said and took off her plain, sensible, brown dress. The naked girl was curious. "Now why is this dress heavy?" she asked. "It is the weight of other people's opinions. I enjoy studying and working and so others call me many unkind names. If I wear anything in the fashion I am told that I am a Boff and shouldn't look so trendy." "I don't want this dress," said the naked girl and handed it back, but the clever girl dropped it on the pile of other clothes and joined in the argument about who had the hardest time.

Soon a poor girl came along the road and offered the naked girl her jumper. "It's second hand but it will keep you warm."
"This jumper is also heavy," said the naked girl.
"Ah I have a hard time being poor. I get all my clothes from charity shops and my clothes never look new or are in fashion. I always walk as though I have a weight on my shoulders and never join in with others in case they see how shabby I look." "I don't want this jumper," said the naked girl, and put it on the growing pile.

A beautiful young teenage boy walked by and stopped to listen to the argument. He saw the naked girl and said, "Let me protect you. Take my trousers and top, they will keep you warm and you'll look great." He took off his clothes to reveal his fine muscles and perfect suntan. But the naked girl said, "I don't need protecting and your clothes are heavy." The boy replied, "I must be attractive, so I have no real friends as I spend my time making myself look good. I have no time for others unless I need an audience and my clothes must show off my body."
"These will not do either," she said and dropped the clothes on the pile.

A boy walked by with a tee shirt that had a picture of his favourite television programme on. "Take my tee shirt," he said and took it off and handed it to her.
"This is just a simple tee shirt but it is very heavy too," said the naked girl.

"That is because it carries the image of a television programme that takes all my time away. I sit at home watching television and I do not think for myself. I don't get any exercise and I don't know what to do when there is nothing on that I want to watch. I don't know how to make my life interesting and I live in a world that is not real."
The naked girl threw the tee shirt on the pile and the television boy joined in the argument as to who had the most difficult life.

The young people argued beside the naked girl far into the night. At some point the argument turned from self-pity to blame upon the other. As each experienced the pointed finger of the others they began to see that there were things about her or his clothes that were worthy and good. There were things that they were proud of.

"I know how to walk tall and feel good about myself," said the beautiful teenager. "Teach me that and I will teach you how to sit unnoticed in a crowd when you want to," said the television boy. "I know how to tell what something is worth by looking at it and feeling it," said the rich boy. "Oh, teach me that and I will teach you how to be thrifty and make something simple look good," said the poor girl.

New life sprang up amongst the young people each of them learning from the other and understanding new values within themselves. And they fashioned for themselves new garments out of the clothing that had piled up at the side of the road, each unique and sharing parts of each.

As the young people taught and worked, the naked girl got up and walked to the next intersection east of them; and sat down.

Adapted from '**The Parable Of The Naked Lady**'
by Anne Spurgeon, in 'Womanguides'

THINGS TO DO

Welcoming the New

Housework of any kind is much more fun if you do it with friends. How about inviting some friends round to help you spring clean? You don't have to do the huge jobs with your friends if you don't want to, but you can work out a list of several things that need doing to clear your space to welcome in Lady Spring and then end your activities with a Potluck dinner, everyone bringing some food to share or bringing one of the courses.

This is a good time to consider what you can give to charity. We have one charity near home and we support one overseas. We don't give much money to them but we help in what ways we can.

This is also the time of year that some people like to put their candles away until the nights begin to draw in again. We sometimes bundle our candles up and tie them with ribbon and give thanks for the light they give. We have a special candle drawer. We use candles all through the year but we use a lot more in winter. This is also the time of year, if you make your own, to make your candles for the coming year.

As we sense the air stir and new life about us it is good to try to get out and be part of nature stirring.

Craft Ideas

Suns

Simple suns can be made in many different ways. Here are some ideas.

Tissue Paper Sun

You will need
- bright, sun coloured tissue paper
- scissors
- glue

(For illustrations see Tissue Paper Stars page 40). Cut 16 rectangular pieces (10 x 3.7cm / 4" x 1½" or what ever size you want your final sun to be). Fold the sheets lengthways and unfold them again.
Fold the four corners in to the centre line so that a point is made above and below. You may want to stick the corners down with a bit of glue.

From the top point fold the two sides once again to the centre line. Fold again (this is one more fold than in the stars).

To stick them together start with 8 points making up a complete star shape, then stick the next eight in-between the first eight until you have a sixteen pointed sun. You can experiment with your sticking together, but if you have made each point very small the job will be very fiddly.

Rose Window Sun

You will need
- yellow, orange, white or red card
- scissors
- glue
- white tissue paper
- sun coloured tissue paper
- thread if hanging

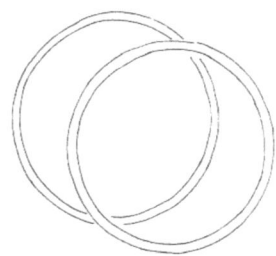

Cut out two circular frames from the card.
Cut out several circles very slightly smaller in diameter, one of which should be white, from the tissue paper. (For ours we used yellows in varying shades and started with the darkest one.)
Keep the white circle whole; this will be your background.
Take one circle and fold it in half. Now fold it in half again. Now fold one side back to the centre, turn over and do the same. This leaves you with an eight-sided cone shape. (Fold again if you want finer rays.)

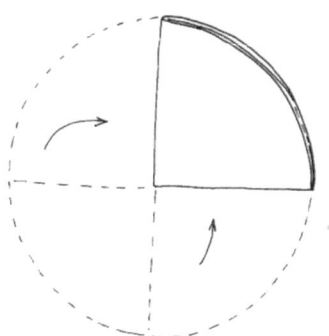

Holding the shape with the point at the bottom carefully cut out a design that looks like the sun's rays. Do this by leaving a point at the top when you have finished cutting.

When you have done this for all the coloured circles giving each one a different cut out shape, glue them gently together onto one of the card frames, starting with the white circle. If you are hanging them glue a piece of thread onto the frame. Glue the second frame on the top.

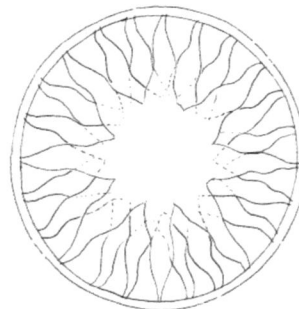

This idea is also very effective with no frame. In this version you won't need the white circle, just stick the suns together in the centre. If you are using transparent glue, dot a little on the rays to stick some of them together.

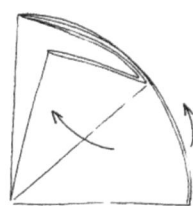

Glass Paint Suns

For these you can use a glass jar or a simple small picture frame with the backing removed so that when you hang it up you can see through it. (Replace the backing with a cardboard frame or a surround from another frame the same size). You can also paint on the inside of a glass picture frame and leave it as it is.

You will need
- glass jars or frames
- gold relief outline
- glass paints
- paint brushes
- white spirit or cleaning fluid
- night-light

Using a gold relief outline (available in tubes with a very fine nozzle so that it's fairly easy to draw a neat line) draw the outline of your sun onto the glass, making sure that all your shapes link up to make solid sections.
Use your glass paints in bright, sunny colours to fill your sun in.
Put a night-light or tea light in the jar or hang your frame up by a window.

Mosaic Suns

For these collect pieces of cellophane paper from sweet wrappings or food wrappings or use tissue paper. We used to enjoy collecting sweet wrappings of all kinds and using them to build up a mosaic.
Either stick your paper onto card in the shape of a sun or cut the card out in a shape first and cover it with shiny paper.

The lovely gold paper on the inner wrapper of chocolate bars does very well. You can also use the glass from a small picture frame as in the glass paint sun instead of card.

Stick Sun

For this you can use straws, sticks or strips of stiff card. If you use sticks you will have to cut a small nick in the centre of your stick so that the centre of your sun sits together. If you are using straws cut them along one side and press them open (if you are using natural straw you will need to soak them and press them open). You can also just flatten them without cutting them open.

You will need
- straws or sticks
- sharp scissors
- gold or natural thread

Cut your sticks or straws into lengths depending on the size of your sun. Lay four crosswise on top of each other making an eight-pointed star shape.

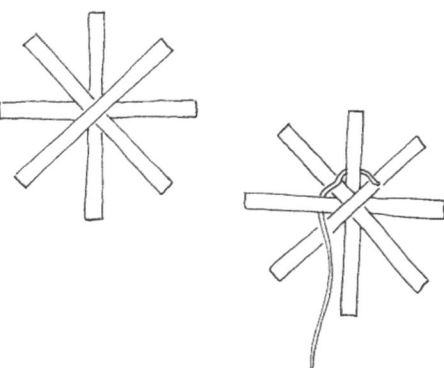

Hold them in place at the centre with one hand and weave a thread round the straws taking it first over the topmost straw, then under the next, then over the one after that and so on.
Finally tie the two ends of thread together behind the star shape.
Make another eight-pointed star shape in the same way and then fix this one to the first one using the same binding method.

You can cut the first binding away if you want to.
Trim the tips.

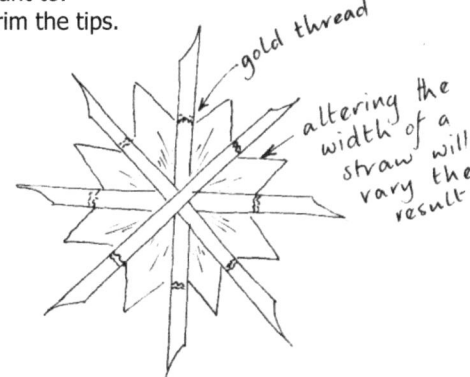

gold thread

altering the width of a straw will vary the result

Other ideas

The sun motif can be used for many different ideas. For example: -
Jewellery
Fimo models
Papier-mâché models (see page 34)
Rag rug (see page 32)
Patchwork (see page 30)

Another representative of the beautiful colours of fire is the fire windsock banner.

Windsock banner

You will need
- a narrow tube of heavy card. (I use the inside of carpet rolls that I got from our resource centre)
- a length of string
- glue
- a stick about a metre long (depending on how tall you are) for example a bamboo stick from garden centres
- a selection of brightly coloured ribbons or strips of material about 1 to 2 metres / 3 to 6 feet long, again depending on how tall you are.

Attach the ribbons to the card tube by wrapping them around it once or twice and gluing it letting a long end hang down (see diagram). Continue until the whole tube is covered.
Tie a length of the string to the sides of the tube then attach the middle of the string to the stick as in the diagram. You now have a brightly coloured banner that can be used in processions at festivals or parties or can be hung in the garden or indoors.
They can be dangerous if used to swing around near people's heads, some supervision may be needed with more boisterous children (and adults!).

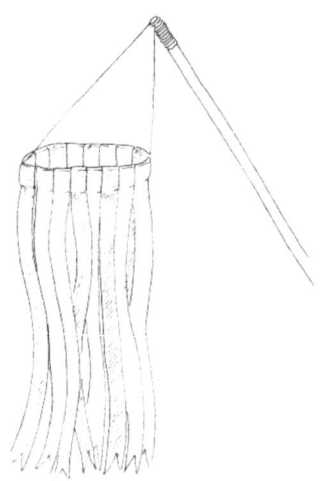

Potato Prints

One year a very creative woman looked after my friend Ruth's son Michael. She took photographs of the lovely time they had together, put them in a scrapbook and got Michael to help her decorate it with pictures and potato prints. Another friend, Jenny, has used potato prints to make a pattern all around the walls of her kitchen.

You will need

- a large potato cut in half
- a sharp craft knife
- paper or card
- paints.

Cut a simple design on the cut face of the potato so that the pattern you want to come out is sticking out.
Cover this with paint and stamp onto your paper or card. We have collected all sorts of pastry cutters in different shapes and have used those to give us some designs. Make sure you clean the potato in between colours so that you keep the colours clean.

One year we made Winter Solstice cards with potato prints of a little robin on a branch. We put them away carefully in the hope that we would find them again at the end of the year. I never did find out what happened to them!

Wind Chimes

Wind chimes can be made from anything that will make a noise when it is hit. We have several around the house but they are not all in draughts so it is not as noisy at it would seem. You can use tubes of metal – experiment to see what sound you like – or wooden tubes or material like large bamboo shoots. We also have a pottery one in the shape of flying birds (not home made but inspiring).

You will need
- tubes or objects that make a pleasant sound when hit
- fishing wire or strong thread
- piece of wood to suspend the tubes from

For the best sound the tubes need to be hung by making a small hole, one third of the way down on either side of the tube, and suspending it with very fine string or cord.
When you have several you can suspend them from a wooden circle or piece of driftwood. They will either knock together in the wind or you can suspend something in the middle of them made of wood (see diagram) so that each note sounds individually.

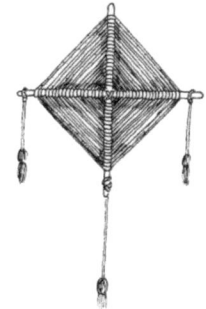

Eye Of Light

These ancient symbols are said to bring good luck and harmony and keep off evil. You can make these in any size and use any sort of material or thread, like wool, embroidery cotton, strips of material, strips of plastic etc. You will need two sticks of equal size. I have used anything from cocktail sticks to garden cane. My friend Rae once used branches about 2 metres in length and hung it up on her wall!

You will need
- sticks of any size
- thread or wool

First tie the sticks into an equal armed cross, then, beginning at the centre (traditionally a bright colour like red, but I use any colour depending on the colour scheme) wind the wool over each arm in turn.

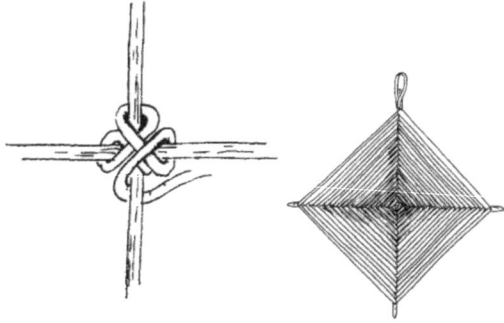

Continue until you reach almost the end of your sticks and then tie off. I sometimes decorate the ends of the cross with pompoms or smaller eyes.

In China, March 8th is known as **Mother Earth Day**. Dating back to the Sung dynasty, Mother Earth Day pays homage to the earth herself. Candles are placed in an area as offerings along with rice, water chestnuts and white almonds. Traditionally these are left in three bowls, each bearing a stick of incense to carry the gift to the Goddess. One activity, which is good to do with the whole family, is to make a papier-mâché model of the earth and as you put the layers on let each person voice their wishes for the earth.

Papier-mâché Earth

You will need
- a small ball or piece of paper screwed up into a ball
- strips of paper
- wallpaper paste or PVA glue
- paint

Cover each strip of paper well with the glue and place it on the ball, building the shape up until you have a larger ball shape.
Leave to dry somewhere where it will not get a flat side, perhaps supported on an eggcup or small bowl.
Once the ball is dry decorate or paint it to look like the earth in what ever way you like.

Boats

In France in early April, the children along the streams that feed the Rhine begin launching small boats with candles for masts. Each candle represents the happiness of life's journey. The boats transport good fortune and good wishes to any child who later finds a vessel and brings it ashore.
Boats can be made from anything that will float! Make sure your boats are attractive and water repellent if you are going to float them down a river or stream as we have

enough litter and pollution in our rivers without more being added.

One idea is to make the boat from lollypop sticks and waterproof glue. PVA is waterproof once it is dry (although you had better test this theory first). Think what good wishes you want to go with the boat and place a small night-light or small votive candle inside before you set it off.

Another idea is to use half an orange. Take out the fruit leaving you with a skin shell. Take off the metal case of a night light and put it in the middle. That way the finished boat is bio-degradable.

You may be able to find a way of writing your good wishes and putting them in the boat so that the water does not wash them away.

Lambs

You will need
- fleece or cotton wool
- thread
- scissors
- needle
- glue (optional)

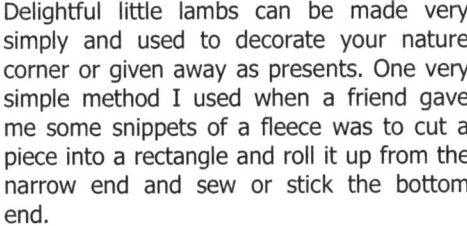

Delightful little lambs can be made very simply and used to decorate your nature corner or given away as presents. One very simple method I used when a friend gave me some snippets of a fleece was to cut a piece into a rectangle and roll it up from the narrow end and sew or stick the bottom end.

I then tied a thread around one end about a third of the way in to make a head and then trimmed it into a little lamb shape.

It is also possible to make a lamb out of cotton wool. Make sure you have a good amount of cotton wool and roll it around until you have a small, fat sausage shape. Tie the shape up in the same way as for the fleece and then tease the wool out into shape.

Dough Rings

We have always enjoyed making bread together and in spring we like to have flowers in the house so here is a recipe for a dough ring to put around a vase of beautiful spring flowers.

Make dough using the following ingredients

500g/1lb flour
½ tablespoon yeast dissolved in
300cc /10fl ozs lukewarm milk
50g /1 ¾ oz hard butter
½ tablespoon salt
3 tablespoons sugar
½ tablespoon aniseed

Keep about 100g/ 4 ozs of flour back and put rest into bowl. Make a hole in the middle and pour the yeast mixture into it. Stir from the middle outwards taking in some of the flour to make a sloppy paste.

Cut the butter up into very thin slices and lay these on to this yeast-mixture. Sprinkle the salt, sugar and aniseed over the butter. Put the bowl into a plastic bag and allow the mixture to rise to twice its volume at room temperature; this can take twenty minutes or more.

Take half of the flour, which you have kept back. Sprinkle it over the mixture with the salt, sugar, aniseed and the butter, which in the meantime has become soft. Empty this loose dough on to the board, which has been sprinkled with flour, and knead it (not too long) until it no longer sticks to your hands and feels firm but still soft and elastic. Knead the dough with the heel of your hand giving it a quarter of a turn now and again.

Put the dough back into the bowl, place in a fridge or cool place, and allow it to rise to about twice its volume. This will take three to four hours. Cold dough can be shaped better.

Divide the risen dough into three portions and roll these out into strips the thickness of your thumb and about three feet (1 metre) long. Make a plait of the three strips. Lay the plait in the form of a wreath on the baking tray and finish off the end-piece as neatly as possible. Place a greased jam-jar inside the wreath to ensure that the centre remains hollow. Cover it all with a plastic sheet and allow to rise to twice its volume. **Remove the jam-jar before baking!**

Pre heat the oven at gas mark 6 / 400° F / 200° C. Bake for about 30 minutes, bottom rack. Before serving sprinkle the wreath with icing-sugar and place a vase with flowers in the centre.

Planting and Sprouting

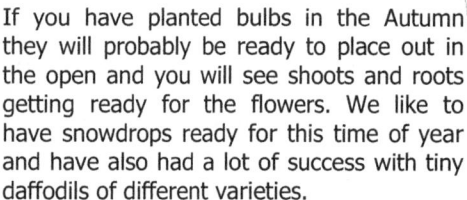

If you have planted bulbs in the Autumn they will probably be ready to place out in the open and you will see shoots and roots getting ready for the flowers. We like to have snowdrops ready for this time of year and have also had a lot of success with tiny daffodils of different varieties.

We like to germinate little alfalfa seeds to eat in our salads. It is good to eat sprouted seeds, as they are the richest source of naturally occurring vitamins known and have been used for almost 5,000 years as a source of high quality food. They also contain proteins fats and carbohydrates plus vitamins and minerals. A teaspoonful of alfalfa seeds will produce half a pound of sprouts and they are one of my daughter's favourite sprouted seeds. We have tried lots of different ones with some success and one favourite recipe is for a sprouted chickpea hummus.

Sprouted Hummus

2 cups or two handfuls of sprouted chickpeas (sprouted for two to three days)
juice of one large lemon
I teaspoon vegetable bouillon powder
3 tablespoon tahini
if you like garlic add one clove – if not, add ½ to 1 teaspoon of ground cumin

Put all the ingredients into a food processor or blender and blend thoroughly with enough water to make it the right consistency for your taste. You can add chopped chives as an option.

This is really delicious and really good for you! I have sometimes made hummus with yoghurt added in (2 dessertspoons of live yoghurt); it gives it a lighter feel.

Spring Bunny Biscuits

100g/4 ozs butter
100g/4 ozs caster sugar
1 egg, beaten
few drops vanilla essence
50g/2 ozs desiccated coconut
100g/4 ozs plain flour
100g/4 ozs ground almonds
pinch salt
½ tsp baking powder

Prepare your baking sheets with greaseproof paper or greasing the surface and put your oven to Gas mark 4/350F/180C.

Beat the butter and sugar together until creamy and beat in the egg and vanilla. Stir in the coconut and ground almonds.

Sift the flour, salt and baking powder and fold into the mixture. Kneed the mixture into a soft dough and roll out about 5cm (¼") thick. Cut out bunny shapes and place on baking tray.

Cook in the oven for about 15 minutes until lightly brown. Allow to cool and dust with a light coating of icing sugar.

Brigit's crosses

Here is one way to make a Brigit's Cross.

You will need
- reeds, straws or construction paper.
- string or ribbon (optional)

Begin by bending two pieces in their middles to form loops. (This will be done with each piece as you make the cross.) Link them together as shown. Turn the pieces so they lie flat and form a right angle. This is the base.

Bend another piece and loop it over the two legs of the last piece you put on. Continue until the cross is the size you want. Tie the ends together with string, reed, straw or ribbon and trim.

The cross can be hung over your heath if you have one to protect the house from lightening, fire and storm and the family from illness.

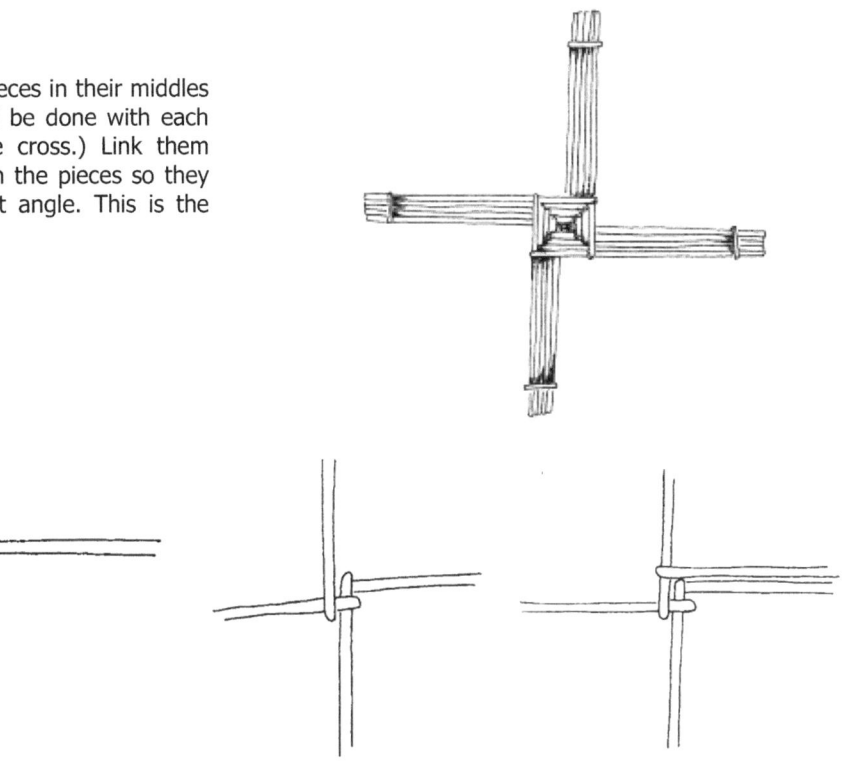

Next bend another piece and loop it over one of the two base pieces. Both legs of the loop in the new piece pass over both legs of the base piece. Pull it tight and hold it in place.

Candles

There are many ways to make candles. One of my favourites is using sand moulds.

Sand Mould Candle

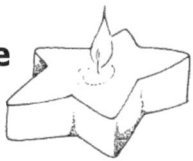

You will need
- damp sand (in a container if you are doing this indoors.)
- an object to make the shape in the sand
- wax
- candle wick
- a stick or pencil

Make a shape in your sand by pressing something into it like a small bowl, a candle, your hand, a star shaped box etc.

Take the object out and you will now have your mould. Using a pointed object, like a skewer or matchstick, press the wick into the sand. (This will be the wick that will be lit.)

Tie the other end of the wick to a small stick or pencil and rest it on the top of the sand as in illustration.

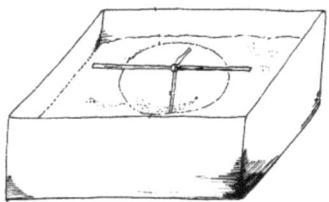

Melt the wax and pour it into the mould. Leave to dry. (For a different effect, drop small pieces of solid wax into the mould before adding the melted wax.)

Crowns of Light

See how many different ways you can make a circle of light as a symbolic headdress for the Goddess. I like to make wreaths to hang up at this time of year, especially ones that will hold candles. You can get so many different shapes of candles that it is easy to come up with something creative that will hold them in a wreath to hang up in your home, perhaps over the dining table. Here is one idea but the design ideas are endless.

Chandelier

You will need
- foliage with long thin twigs
- around 8 night light cases
- ivy or leaves
- flowers or berries to decorate
- candles
- ribbon
- florist's wire or something similarly flexible
- scissors

Remove some of the leaves from the twigs and carefully bend the twigs into a circle shape, binding them with florist's wire as you go. Work until you have a firm base of twigs that can hold its shape.

Make a small hole in the bottom of each night light case and pass a length of wire (about 40cms/16" long) through it. Bend the wire around inside of the case and bend over the edge, bringing it back under base. Securely bind each case onto the chandelier base with wire, so they cannot move.

To hang the chandelier, attach the ends of two lengths of wire securely at equal intervals on the base.

Hang the chandelier so it's easier to work. If your twigs do not have leaves bind short lengths of leaf stems or ivy along the inside of twigs with wire, then around the outside, covering most of the base with wire and more ivy so that it is well covered. Then bind in small bunches of flowers or berries so they hang off the chandelier slightly. Ensure that all the leaves and berries are attached securely.

Melt the ends of the candles slightly and push into place in the metal cases. Cut a length of ribbon long enough to cover the hanger and tie to the base.

Butterfly Garden

If you can cope with caterpillars sampling your cabbages, you may like to create a butterfly garden. It is possible for us all to do something positive to preserve the wildlife by providing a little oasis of food and shelter. The smallest garden can, for very little financial outlay or physical effort, be turned into a mini nature reserve and the gardener can be assured that any efforts will be amply repaid.

Food must be offered to passing butterflies, in the form of nectar-bearing flowers, and once the eggs have been laid caterpillar food must also be available.

Plants for caterpillar food are:

ash, beech, birch, blackthorn, bramble, buckthorn, burdock, cabbage, carrot, cherry, clover, dandelion, dock, elm, fennel, gorse, hawthorn, hop, horseradish, lime, nettle, oak, plum, poplar, privet, scabious, sorrel, spurge, thistle, willow, willowherb.

Some of the plants for butterflies are:

ageratum, alyssum (white), arabis, aubrietia, bluebell, buddleia (butterfly bush), campion, candytuft, cineraria, clover, comfrey, cowslip, daisy, dandelion, everlasting pea, foxglove, globe thistle, golden rod, heather, hebe, heliotrope, honeysuckle, lavender, lilac, mallow, marigold, marjoram, michaelmas daisy, petunia, phlox, polyanthus, primrose, sea holly, sedum, sweet rocket, sweet william, thrift, thyme, valerian, verbena, wallflower.

The single headed flowers are the ones that insects and butterflies can easily land on and get to the nectar. It is possible that, if you are looking after your garden well, you will have a lot of pesky creatures helping themselves to lunch as a well-tended garden is like a supermarket to them. If your garden is large enough, don't worry too much about plants being eaten. If you have enough to go round, enjoy the flowers that are doing their best to attract attention.

Near our house there is an allotment for young gardeners. Children start to take an interest in growing things at a very early age and each year there is an award for the best child's allotment.

Song for Imbolc

Another round. A light, bright song about the coming of the new year just before spring.

H.Royall

Deep, deep, deep with in, The spark I am, The spark I am,

Dream, dream, dream, dream, The spark I am, The spark I am.

Eostar
Renewal

EOSTAR & THE VERNAL EQUINOX
(21st – 22nd March)

Primroses and violets stay with us from Imbolc and purple lupines line the mountains in the deserts of California. In the flowering seed sleeps the knowledge and promise of maturity. If the snow has gone we can see the fields greening and soon it will be time for the blackthorn to blossom and the delicate pinks and whites of the orchard blossoms to line our pathways. It is time to celebrate the equality of light and dark. In times gone by, as soon as the soil began to warm up and be workable the seed corn and barley would have been sown by hand. Among it would be the special ears of corn saved as the corn doll, symbol of the corn god sacrificed at harvest-tide.

This is the Vernal Equinox, and the season of spring reaches its apex, halfway through its journey from Imbolc to Beltaine. The Great Mother Goddess, who has returned to her virgin aspect at Imbolc, welcomes the young sun god's embraces and conceives a child. The child will be born nine months from now, at the next Winter Solstice. (The old folk name for the Vernal Equinox is 'Lady Day').

With the lunar aspect of the Goddess we remember the descent of the Goddess into the Underworld for three days, the time when the moon is dark and hidden from our view. We can then celebrate the next full moon (the Eostar) when the Goddess returns from her sojourn into the Land of Death. For some this is the time to celebrate the Hand-fasting, a sacred marriage between Goddess and God, the ultimate Great Rite although the British custom is to transfer this to Beltaine, when the climate is more suited to outdoor celebrations! Though I have placed the telling of the Descent stories in Samhaine they also belong here with the ascent back to the Upper World at spring.

Easter was taken from the name of a Teutonic lunar Goddess, Eostre (from whom we also get the name of the female hormone, oestrogen). Eostar falls on the Vernal Equinox full moon. For some people there is confusion about dates at this time of year. Eostar is a lunar holiday, honouring a lunar Goddess, at the Vernal Full Moon. Eostar is reserved for the nearest festival. In our family we are not so specific and celebrate this season whenever we feel like enjoying some spring activities.

In her book 'The Spiral Dance' Starhawk talks of a basket of story eggs – each painted egg is taken out of the basket and a story is told. One of the eggs is painted half black and half gold to represent the balance of the equinox. In Ceisiwr Serith's book 'The Pagan Family' he suggests the fun of an egg fight. Each person chooses an egg. Two people then face the small ends of their eggs towards each other. One of them hits the other's egg with her own. When one person's cracks, he turns his around and has another chance with the other side. (He does not say whether this is with raw eggs or hard-boiled!)

For several years my daughter and I (and any friends who had dropped in at the time) would take our bell sticks and go for a walk out along the wooded paths and as we went we would bang the ground with our sticks calling, "Wake up earth! Wake up earth!" and skip around to wake all the sleeping nature. It is a long time since we have felt able to pick the wild flowers that blossom at this time so we content ourselves with a wonderful spring walk and leave the flowers for others to enjoy. If we want to deck our home with primroses and violets and early daffodils we have to grow them ourselves.

We focus now on new life and the return of hope after a long winter and find ways to celebrate the emerging life. Following the cleaning of the home at Imbolc we like to invite friends round to batik eggs. This is a wonderful activity that we have done for several years. I was taught the traditional Ukrainian egg batik method from a friend, Helen, in Bedford nearly twenty years ago and for the last five years I have gathered together my friends, decorated eggs and shared food and gossip (the noble and much maligned art of news sharing).

Goddess for Eostar

Brigit

Brigit is the Fire Goddess, dressed in bright reds and yellows, riding on a fiery golden arrow. She is the ancient triple Fire Goddess presiding over fire, beauty and all the arts and crafts.

(In Kathy Jones' book 'The Ancient British Goddess' it is suggested that the name Brigit originally meant Goddess and was given to all Irish and British Goddesses. The Irish form means 'high' or 'exalted'. Brigit comes from brea-saigit' – fiery arrow.)

She is also known as The White Goddess and bringer of light. Brides who wear white at their wedding represent her. Brigit is also the Goddess of healing at the sacred well. There are many Bridewells all over Britain where her healing waters can still be drunk. She is also Goddess of the Hearth-fire, both in the home and in the smithy. The Hearth-fire was the source of light, heat and warm food – the heart of every home.

Her symbols are fiery reds and yellows, snowdrops, mirrors, spinning wheels and the Holy Grail. We make brightly coloured eyes of light to decorate our windows at this time of year. We also place a beautiful wall-hung candleholder near our stove and we light a candle whenever we cook to ask her to bless the food as we prepare it.

LITTLE RAINBOW

In a village west of the moon and north of the stars, you will find some gentle people who loved the land they lived in. They would celebrate with joy, knowing that all around them was overflowing abundance and peace. Fishes danced in rainbows in the water and birds sang in harmony with the seasons and all was well.

One day in early spring, a day to be remembered, it was the time for the son of the Dancers Lodge to be betrothed to the daughter of the Wise Woman. Bright Sunlight was tall and strong and his eyes knew laughter and deep joy. Waterfall was as dancing and beautiful as her name. The two of them came together with great feasting and celebration, singing and dancing and all the people rejoiced. The children brought gifts and together the people of the village built a new house for the two of them to live in.

The celebrations went on for three days and nights, until the Wise Woman declared that the quiet time had come for the couple to be alone and enjoy their coupling. So the people went back to their gardens to work and play and gossip and laugh as the seasons unfolded.

Several moons later the young couple were proud to announce the imminent arrival of a baby and, as Imbolc sprang into new life all around them, a beautiful little boy was born. The whole village was excited and delighted and came to the young couples' home to visit the new child … and when they went in to bring their gifts and to see the little baby they were amazed.

He was horrible.

He was so ugly with his tiny little face screwed up into a furious ball, and his tiny little voice letting out the most horrendous, angry cry that they didn't know what to do. They left their gifts, said how lovely the new baby was and quickly made their exit.

Bright Sunlight and Waterfall were beside themselves with worry. Nothing they tried could stop the crying. The baby cried all day and all night. Soon nobody would visit and the two new parents were left on their own to cope.

It happened that the Wise Woman did not live among the people, preferring as she did to live a little way up the side of the mountain that overlooked the village. One day Bright Sunlight said the only thing he could think of to do that would help was to go and pay a visit to his Goddess Mother, the Wise Woman.

He packed food, for he thought he might be away for some days, and said goodbye to his wife and a hasty goodbye to the baby, and said that he would be back as soon as he could bring help or find an answer to their troubles.

It was early morning when he set out to cross the river and the Sunlight shone brightly over the mountaintop and into the peaceful valley. Bright Sunlight felt relieved and light-hearted as he made his way upwards. He noticed that as he moved silently through the forest bright patches of sunlight played on the new leaves of the lime trees and wherever the willow bent her head to reach the waters, little ripples of sunlight danced away from the branches. If Bright Sunlight felt any guilt about leaving his young bride to deal with their son while he walked in peace, enjoying the newness of the season, he tucked it conveniently away behind the thought that soon he would see his Goddess Mother and she would know all the answers to their problems.

The day wore on and Bright Sunlight found himself trekking up the last few metres of the steep mountainside to come to the peaceful cave where the Wise Woman lived. Outside there was a spring where Bright Sunlight took some drops of the water and gave thanks to the Goddess for being with him on his journey and bringing him safely to his destination. The Wise Woman came out of the cave when she heard him and greeted him fondly.

"Bright Sunlight, you look tired and pale. Is it so hard to look after a young baby when the weather is so fine and bright and you have a whole village to help you, or are you ill?" She said all this with a twinkle in her eye for she knew why Bright Sunlight had come to see her.

"Lady, I am pleased to see you looking so well. I bring greetings from the village people, my friends and from my beloved mate, Waterfall." "Good, all then is well. Sit down Bright Sunlight and tell me why you have come." And Bright Sunlight told the Wise Woman his story about how the baby was restless and cried the whole time and would not give either of them any peace. When he had finished the Wise Woman thought for a while and then said, "You tell me much about your son but you have not once mentioned his name. What do you call him?"

Bright Sunlight looked startled. "Why we have not yet named him. We are too busy trying to calm him down. We call him Noisy or Fretful or Nuisance usually."

The Wise Woman looked intently at the young man. "Do you not know the power of a name my boy?" she asked him quietly. "Do you not know that the name you are called by your friends and family is the name you become? How would it be if I called you Nuisance? Would you have the courage to come and see me in your troubles? And how would it be if I called you Stupid? Would you then achieve such brave and powerful things as you do?" Bright Sunlight, the brave, bright young man looked sheepishly down at his hands and knew that she was right. Hadn't he, only this morning, walked from his village rejoicing in the sunlight and knowing that he was as bright and as strong and as beautiful as that very sunlight?

"What must I do, Goddess Mother?" he asked. "You must find your son a name. That is all" She looked at her hand-fast son and wondered, not for the first time, why such simple things were not obvious to him.
Bright Sunlight stayed a while to talk with the Wise Woman and share some of his food with her and then went to look for a name for his little son.

It was evening when he left her. He would not stay for now he knew what he had to do he was eager to get on. First he had to go down the side of the mountain. There he met a wolf who was nearly blind. He sat and talked awhile with the old wolf and asked if he could give him a name for his little son. The wolf listened to Bright Sunlight talking about his little boy. "He is tiny and usually bright red and very noisy." "But what do you see in his eyes?" asked the old wolf.

"When for a moment, he stops crying, he looks at his mother and there is such a bond, even though his mother is so tired. It would be nice to call him something that fits with his mother, like Little Streamlet." "That would be good. Think how lucky he is, and you are, to have the use of your eyes, and name him well young Sunlight."

Bright Sunlight thanked the wolf and went on his way. Soon he was in the forest where he met a poor little squirrel who could not use her hands properly and so was unable to pick up nuts to eat. Bright Sunlight sat with her a while and shared some of his food. He asked her if she could think of a name for his little boy.

The squirrel listened to Bright Sunlight talking about his little boy. "He is tiny and has beautiful eyes and is very noisy." "But what do you see in his hands?" asked the squirrel. "Ah, his hands are so tiny and strong. When I hold him sometimes he grips me and I can lift him up. He will be strong like his father. It would be nice to call him something that fits with my name, like Little Sunbeam."

"That would be good," said the squirrel. "Remember how lucky you are to have such fine strong limbs and name him well young Sunlight."

Bright Sunlight thanked the squirrel and went on his way. The nearer he came to home the more he looked forward to seeing Waterfall and his little son again. Nearing the end of the forest he came across a most beautiful bird. She was sitting on a branch looking down at Bright Sunlight. "You are looking bright and happy, is your name not Bright Sunlight and are you not looking for a name for your little son?" she chirruped. "I am indeed," he replied, "do you know what I should call him?"

Bright Sunlight sat down at the foot of the tree and the little bird sat on a branch near by. "Tell me about your son," she said. "He is tiny but strong and has beautiful eyes, he has a good strong voice and the raven dark hair of his mother." "And will he be free, as free as the birds to go where he will and know what there is to know?" asked the little bird. "Why I don't know what will be his pathway, I will do what I can to help him." "Then you must name him well." said the bird and flew up into the sky chirruping and singing for the joy of flight.

Bright Sunlight was nearly home now and still he had not thought of a name for his son. "It will come," he thought to himself. He was nearing the river now and bent down by a little waterfall to drink and to fill his water bottle. As he did so he saw a ray of bright sunlight catch the splashing drops from the waterfall and a dazzling rainbow arch across the water. It was gone in a moment but Bright Sunlight, in that moment, knew the name of his son.

Jumping excitedly across the river he ran the rest of the way home and into the house where Waterfall held her son on her lap trying to calm him. Bright Sunlight came over to her, kissed her and took up his son in his arms. Holding him up so he could see his eyes he said, "Hello my son, your name is Little Rainbow." At these words Little Rainbow stopped crying and snuggled into his father's arms and went peacefully to sleep.

From then on Little Rainbow grew to be a favourite child of the village, always interested and bright, loving vibrant colours and showing real skill in the arts. Waterfall and Bright Sunlight lived happily together and when, at next season's Beltaine, they had a daughter they named her straight away.

Adapted from an idea by Jan Morgan Wood

THINGS TO DO

Renewal

Craft Ideas

Ukrainian Egg Batik

Egg decorating has been handed down through generations of the Ukrainian people. They believe that great powers are embodied in the egg and that it symbolises the release of earth from the shackles of winter and the coming of spring with the promise of new life, new hope and prosperity. Legend has it that as long as 'pysanky' (the eggs) are decorated, goodness will prevail over evil throughout the world. Pysanky are not made to be eaten, they are made as gifts and given to guests and friends who visit and they are used as decorations all year round.

In April 1996 we remembered the disaster in Chernobyl of 1986 where still, ten years later, the Ukrainian capital, Kiev, was a forbidden zone surrounded by barbed wire, and Polessky was a forgotten town in constant winter where people were waiting to be moved to new homes and jobs. We concentrated on the hope of new life for these people and gave thanks for the beautiful and fragile gift of the Ukrainian people.

To make a Pysanka you will need
- a white egg (the egg must be fresh or it will not sink in the dye)
- kistky (writing tools)
- beeswax (other wax will not work as well)
- cold water dyes
- white vinegar
- pint size jars with wide mouths and covers
- small brush or cotton swab
- candle and candle holder
- soft tissue or rags
- pencil

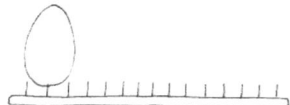

To rest the egg while drying or when not working on it, I have made a simple stand by hammering small tacks into a board about 100cm x 200cm (4" x 8" see diagram).
Prepare the dyes as directed on the packets. Use dyes at room temperature. When not in use store them in the jar with the lid on to stop them evaporating.
Select raw, fresh, clean, smooth white eggs. If you need to wash them do so gently, (do not rub) in a solution of one quart warm water to one tablespoon of white vinegar. (Never use soap or detergent). Leave to dry.
To work your design it is good to be relaxed and rest your arms at the wrist on the working surface in front of you. Hold the egg in one hand and write with the other. Rotate the egg as you work.

Draw your design on the egg very lightly with the pencil. These lines will not show once you have finished. Use long, smooth lines rather than short, sketchy ones.

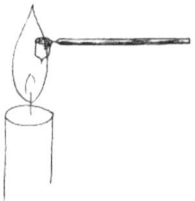

Once your design is complete it is time to heat the kistka. Light your candle and hold the head of the tool over the flame. When hot, scoop a little wax into the funnel of the kistka.

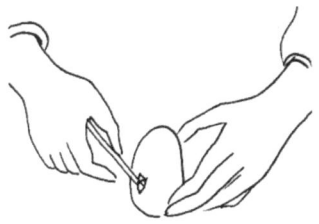

Write over the pencil lines keeping the kistka at right angles with the egg, allowing the wax to flow evenly. As you work the wax will blacken. This is helpful as you will be able to see your lines. Do not over heat, as the wax will drip. As soon as the kistka stops writing smoothly reheat and fill.

Wherever you put wax at this stage will be left white on your finished pysanka.

Next place the egg on the spoon and lower it into the dye. I usually start with yellow but your first colour should be the lightest. You will work towards the darkest.

When the desired colour is obtained (5 to 15 minutes), remove the egg and pat dry with the tissue or rag. Do not rub.

Add more wax with the kistka covering over anything that you want to stay yellow.

Continue in this way until you have completed your design. Green areas like leaves and grass can be added with a small brush or cotton swab. Cover with wax once you have painted it.

Now comes the most exciting part – removing the wax and watching your design come to life! Hold the egg to the side of the candle flame for a few seconds until the wax starts to melt. With a tissue or rag, wipe away the melted wax a small portion at a time.

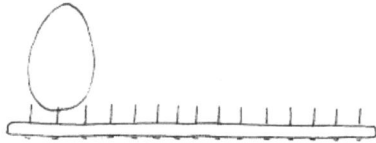

The egg may now be varnished, and placed on the egg rack to dry. Varnish adds protection and lustre.

On the next page the illustrations show a traditional design in various stages.

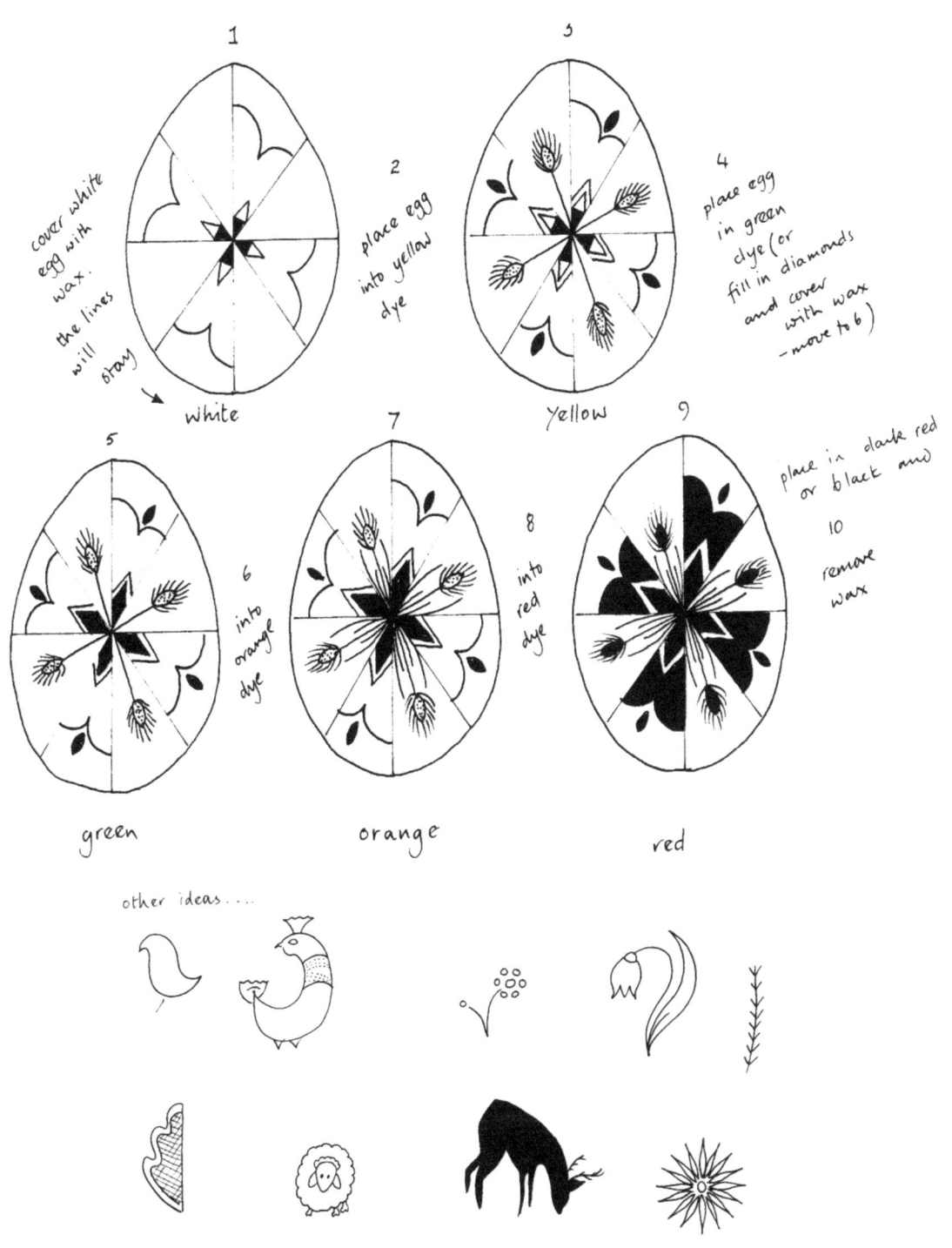

1

cover white egg with wax. the lines will stay ➔

white

2

place egg into yellow dye

3

4

place egg in green dye (or fill in diamonds and cover with wax – move to 6)

yellow

5

green

6

into orange dye

7

orange

8

into red dye

9

place in dark red or black and

10

remove wax

red

other ideas....

74

Marbled Eggs

You will need
- raw eggs
- food colouring
- saucepan
- jam jars
- spoon
- kitchen paper or rags

In a saucepan, hard-boil the eggs, drain and leave to cool.

Gently tap the egg against hard surface so the shell begins to crack all over – be careful not to break the inner membrane.

Fill a jar with cold water (enough to cover the egg) then add food colouring. Leave the egg to soak for at least 30 minutes.

Remove the egg with a spoon, rinse and leave to dry on kitchen paper or rags. Remove the shell to reveal a delicate cobweb of colour.

If you don't compost them keep the eggshells to decorate your May Tree.

Story Egg Basket

You may like to make a story egg basket. Decorate a basket with ribbons and flowers and paint or decorate hard-boiled eggs or use chocolate eggs.

Each time someone draws out an egg they can tell a story about it – or any story. Include an egg that is half black and half gold if you want to, to represent the equal day and night. This could be followed by an egg hunt.

Kites

Kites are a lovely sight in spring and add to the feeling of freedom that spring brings. I have found many designs recently, many on the Internet. Here is one favourite. Dave found this one and tried it with our Woodcraft group. It was very successful and attractive.

You will need
- 24, 20cms / 8" straws
- kite string
- glue stick
- tissue paper
- poster board for template
- scissors, ruler, pencil, protractor

Cut four pieces of string about 11cms / 45" long. Cut four pieces of string about 6.2cms / 25" long.

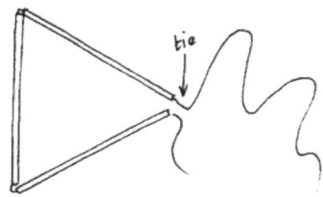

Place three straws on a 11cm / 45" string and tie them in a triangle with one string end very long and the other end short.

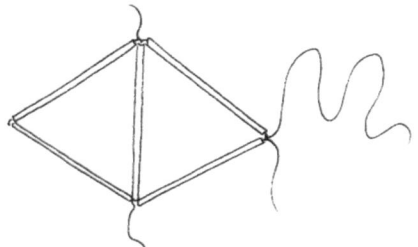

Place two straws on a 6.2cm / 25" string and tie them to the corners of the triangle that do not have the original knot.

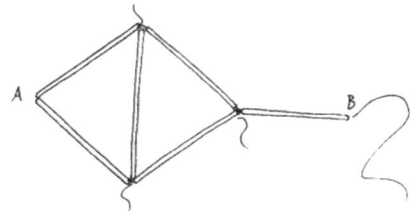

From the poster board cut a template with the following dimensions –

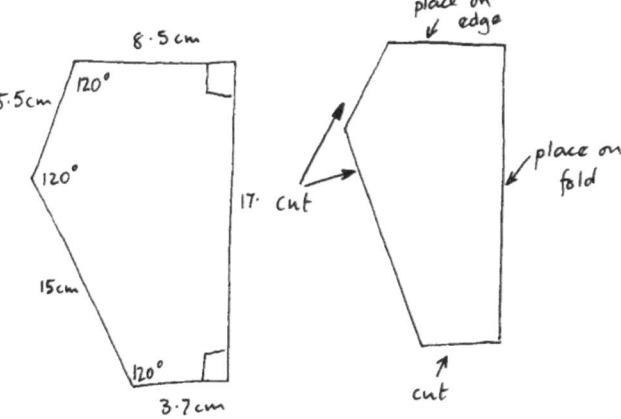

Place one straw on the long end of the original 11 / 45" string and tie it to the free vertex of the other equilateral triangle. Connect A to B

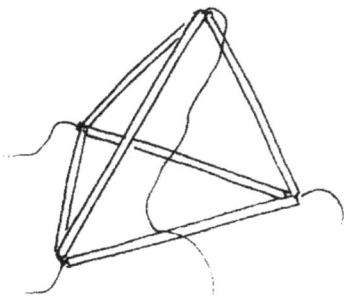

Place the template on the folded corner of tissue and cut where indicated. You will end up with four tissue pieces that look like this.

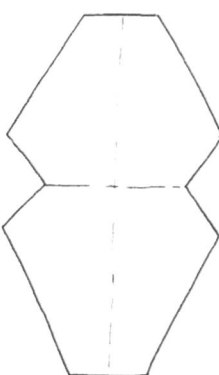

You now have a Tetrahedron. Make three more.

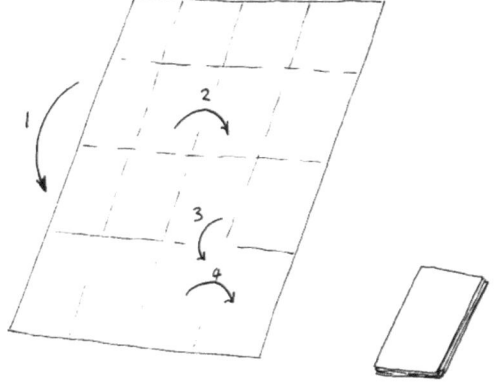

(This is enough for one kite. If you want a multi-coloured kite, fold and cut more tissue.)
Add the tissue pieces to each of the four small straw tetrahedra covering two faces of each.

Once you have the four tetrahedra you will need to cover them with tissue paper. Begin with a full sheet of tissue 5cms x 7.5cms / 20" x 30". Fold it in half 4 times.

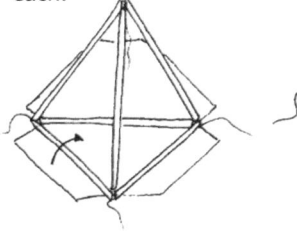

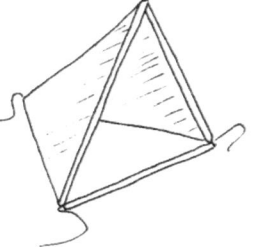

Assemble the kite by using the strings at each vertex. Tie the four tetrahedra together in a larger tetrahedron, as shown, making sure all the tissue faces are facing the same direction, or the kite will not fly. Use extra string at the corners if the kite is a little floppy.

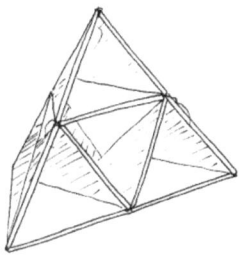

Now attach the bridle. Cut a loop of string about 40cms / 18" long and tie a loop knot at its centre as shown.

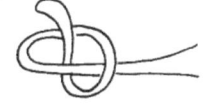

Tie one end of this string to the top of your kite at point A. Tie the other end to point B. The loop should be centred between the two points.

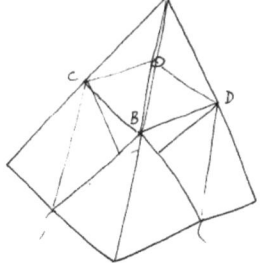

Cut a second length of string about 60cms / 24" long. Tie one end of the string to the kite at point C. Thread another end through the loop knot and tie at point D. Be sure the loop is pulled taught before tying at D. All strings should be taut when pulling out on the loop knot.

Attach your flying string to the loop knot. The kite requires no tail for stable flight.

Knitted Hare

It is so simple to make a little knitted hare and has been one of my daughter's favourites.

You will need
- knitting wool (not too thick)
- knitting needles 3mm (size 2)
- stuffing (e.g. unspun wool)

Knit a square, 1 plain 1 purl about 13cms / 5". Make sure that the knitting is not too tight, as a loosely knitted piece is easier to make into a hare.

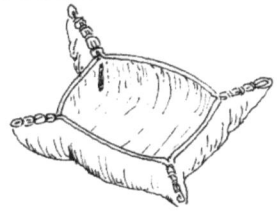

Pinch and sew the four corners together for a good 2cms / 1"; these points are for the legs of the hare.
Gather in a piece between the feet on one side so that the head can be shaped there afterwards.

Sew the belly as far as the hind legs and stuff the animal tightly with the stuffing. Tie a woollen thread tightly round the neck to make the head. Now draw the hind legs under the body to the front and pin them.

Sew up the hindmost seam, sew the legs on under the body, and remove the pins. Tuck the body in a bit so that the rump becomes nice and round. Sew up the whole thing.

Make a little round tail by pinching a bit of the knitting with your fingers and winding some wool round it.

Shape up the hare, stitch the eyes and draw them together.

Finally, knit the ears by casting on three stitches and knit all rows plain. The ears are to be about 40cms / 1½" long. Sew them to the head. The whole hare is about 9cms / 3½" long.

Butterflies

Very uncomplicated butterflies can be made simply by cutting out little tissue paper shapes and tying them onto sticks.

You will need
- tissue paper of different colours
- cotton thread
- a small stick

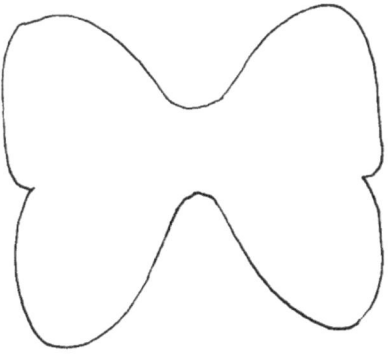

Cut a simple butterfly shape out of the tissue paper. (See template above.) Tie the cotton thread around the centre of the butterfly letting the paper in the centre crinkle up slightly.

Attach the cotton thread to the stick.

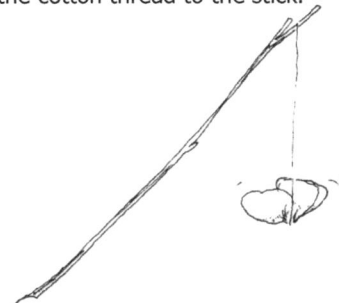

To add variety you can cut a second tissue butterfly, slightly smaller than the first and in a different colour and lay it on top of the first one before you attach the cotton thread.

The same design can be used for hair slides. Attach the butterfly to a hair slide or clip using a small amount of cotton thread.

Squash Paint Butterflies

You will need
- tubes of bright coloured acrylic paint or poster paint
- paper
- scissors
- ruler

Fold one sheet of paper in half and cut into a butterfly shape.

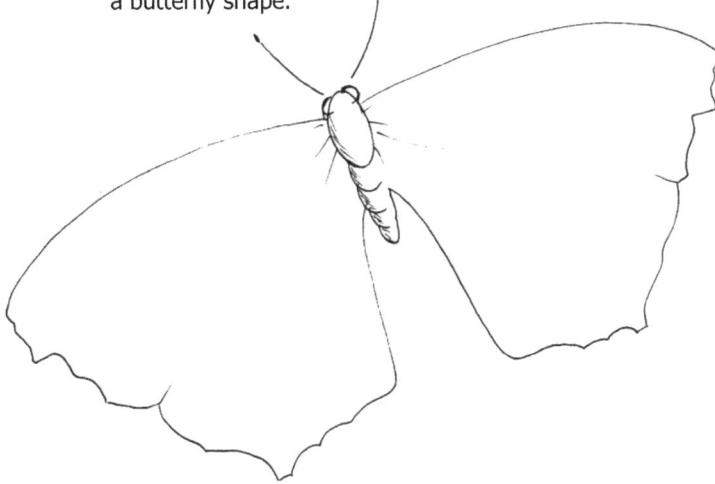

Open the sheet up and on one side squeeze out a little paint. Use several colours.

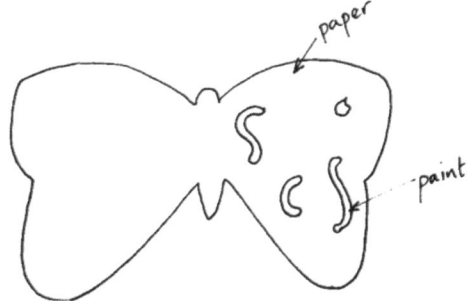

Close the shape up again and press from the centre outwards. You may want to use a ruler or piece of wood for this.

Open the paper and see what a beautiful brightly coloured butterfly you have.

I used this once with a group of young children, telling them how there were once some little caterpillars, as I squeezed out the paint into little caterpillar shapes on the paper, and they ate and ate and ate until they got so full they had to sleep. Then folding the page over I told them how something magic happened while they were asleep. I let the children press the paper down to see if the caterpillars were still there. Then I opened it up and showed them how the caterpillars had all turned into butterflies, which flew away in the sunshine.

Draw String Butterflies

Another way to decorate a butterfly shape is to use inks and string.

You will need
- inks or watered down paint (e.g. water colour)
- very fine string or cotton thread
- pots
- paper
- scissors
- hardback book

Again cut out your butterfly shape from the paper and fold it down the middle. Open out the shape and lay it down on a surface.

Dip the thread into the ink or paint leaving about 10cms / 4" at one end free of paint. Drop the thread onto one half of the paper butterfly, leaving the clean end of the thread off the paper and close the shape. You will need to work quite quickly.

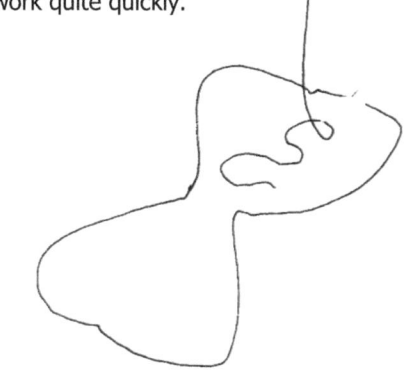

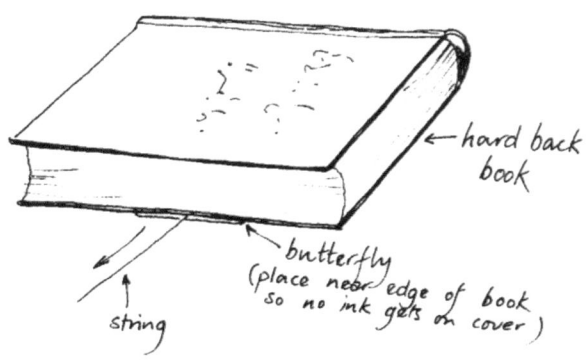

Place the hardback book on top of the butterfly and press it down with one hand while pulling the thread out with the other.

Remove the book and open the butterfly. You should now have a beautiful drawn string shape over the paper. Repeat until you are happy with the design.

Splash Paint Butterflies

If the weather has warmed up enough by then you might like to make a butterfly out of doors, just splashing paint onto the paper by flicking the brush loaded with paint at the paper. It can be done indoors if you are willing to take the risk of paint on the walls!

You will need
- paper
- water based paint, ready diluted
- paintbrushes
- scissors

Cut the paper into butterfly shapes. Dip the paintbrush into the paint and then, holding it at the end, flick the brush at the paper by knocking it in the middle on the finger of your other hand.

You can wet the paper first and the colours will then blend into each other.

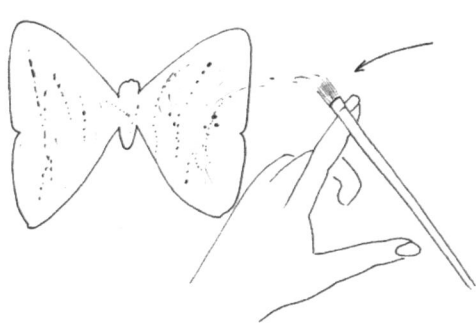

Spring Seeds

Here is a lovely idea to entertain children who drop in as well as your own.

You will need
- egg shells
- potting compost
- seeds

Collect several eggshells and decorate them if you want to. Cut off the tops and add a small drainage hole on the bottom.
Fill the eggs with potting compost, add the seed, and keep moist.
When the seeds are ready to plant out the eggshells make good compost. Crack the shells before planting out.

Chocolate Pecan Pie

This recipe, which my friend Liz gave me, is a real favourite with all the family and one I use for special occasions.

Pastry
275g/10 ozs plain flour
3 level tablespoons cocoa powder
150g/5 ozs butter
2 level tablespoons caster sugar

Filling
200g/7 ozs pecan nuts
3 eggs
225g/8 ozs light brown sugar
220ml/8 fl ozs evaporated milk
50g/2 ozs melted butter

Sift the flour and cocoa powder into a large bowl. Add the diced butter and rub together until you have the consistency of breadcrumbs. Add the sugar. Gradually add 2 – 3 tablespoons of cold water.
Turn the dough onto a floured surface and roll out as for pastry. Put into a greased, fluted, flan tin. Prick the pastry and chill for 1 hour. And then blind bake in the oven, Gas mark 5/375F/190C for 10 minutes.

While this is cooking set aside 50g/2 ozs of the pecan nuts and liquidise or mix together all the filling ingredients. Pour into the flan case and decorate with the remaining pecan nuts.
Cook in an oven Gas mark 3/325F/170C for one hour until set in the centre. This dish can be eaten hot or cold.

Song for Eostar
Nightingale Sing
A three part round

H.Royall

Nigh-tin-gale   sing,   nigh-tin-gale   sing   sing from your heart, sing to my heart

sing   of   free — dom,   nigh — tin — gale   sing.

Beltaine
Time to Play

BELTAINE
(May eve – 30th April)

Beltaine is the glorious season of rich growth when scarcity gives way to plenty and it is time to celebrate Mother Earth in all her gifts. May Day is the call to awaken. It is one of the great celebrations in Europe, celebrated from Ireland to Russia. Finally the winter is over and the cattle are sent to their summer pastures. In times past bonfires would smoulder and the cattle would be cleansed of ticks by being driven through a thick medicinal smoke of burning herbs. Since Beltaine got its name from its bonfires it is the perfect time to have one.

The month of May was always a time of relief in agricultural communities when it was possible to feel the warmth in the air. Young people were allowed out all night to hunt through the woods and coppices for the first branches of flowering hawthorn, and bring them back to decorate their homes. They would also collect the green of the sycamore tree, the wood traditionally used to make love spoons.

> Here we go gathering knots of may,
> Knots of may, knots of may,
> Here we go gathering knots of may,
> On a cold and frosty morning

As the month of May suggests it is the time to bring out the Maypole and join in the traditional dancing around it with ribbons. There is no real evidence that Maypole dancing was a Pagan or Celtic tradition. The Maypole dancing that we know today was brought to England by John Ruskin, a Victorian who ran a Teacher Training College. He had seen the dancing around a pole with ribbons in Italy, brought it back to England, and taught it to his teachers who then went out and taught it to school children. There may well have been May Day dances around a tree that had been decorated with the May branches. These may have been included with the May Day civic dances that were around in the 15th and 16th Centuries but the Puritans frowned on such happy behaviour, linking it with Pagan activities, and tried to put a stop to it. (You may like to find out more about the dances from the website www.kickback.btinternet.co.uk)

Be that as it may, for many the maypole dance is still the symbol of this season, weaving and celebrating the sexuality of male and female together. For others the white maypole lifted high above the ground is the symbol of the white mare of Rhiannon/Aphrodite/Venus who rode onto the land from the ocean to teach us about the sacredness of love between two people. For others it is the weaving of summer warmth and good growth, fertilising the sun power from above with the nourishing earth power below. According to Marian Green in her book 'A Calendar of Festivals' dancing around the maypole represents the tidal patterns of energy being sent down from the sun and the unwinding shows how the power is returned to the sky in a cyclic and unending pattern.

Other rites at this time may include the jumping of the water. A narrow part of a stream can be used to jump over and give thanks for water and hope that there will be enough to feed the land and crops for the growing months. Some may like to jump the cauldron with another person for whom they wish to give thanks. Children love this ritual and jump with family, friends and loved ones, even favourite teddies have been included.

May Day rites also include the Holly and Oak Lords battling for the hand of the maiden who, after her mating, would become the Mother and bring forth the following spring. After this fight, when he is beaten, the Holly Lord retires with his hounds to the Wild Wood to rest until he is recalled at Samhaine. This would take place on May eve. In Cornwall they still tell of the various battles between dark and light, good and evil with Robin Hood, St George and the dragon, or St Michael. Some still have the crowning of the May Queen, a modern version of Maid Marian, the ancient White Lady who could change herself into a deer to hide in the forest, who brought healing water from the secret springs and who cared for all the wild creatures and the forest.

Trees have long been the centre of our celebrations. At this time it is good to decorate the May Tree representing the tree of life. Hang ribbons, flowers and eggshells saved from Eostar on the tree. You may have stayed up all night on May eve making things to decorate your tree (and yourself). Include lots of singing, games and dancing to welcome the summer. Also on May Day those who wanted to look after their skin would be out before sunrise, seeking a patch of dew to bathe their face and eyes.

Many weddings would take place at this time of year, the young couples pledging themselves for 'a year and a day'. To seal their bond they would leap over a bonfire hand in hand. We have chosen this time to write a letter to someone we love or care about, to tell her or him how much s/he is appreciated. It may be someone you have been married to for some time and you wish to renew your vows or express things that you don't often say, or it may be a daughter, son, parent or friend. It could even be someone you would like to know better. We have great fun with our letter writing, which we feel is something of a dying art. We use lovely bright coloured pens and illustrate the letters with drawings or pressed flowers. My daughter is especially fond of the scented pens that are available now. If we don't get round to writing we try to say something special in a 'phone call or when we see the person but a letter is very special so it is always worth making the effort.

Spend time out of doors, have picnics, play outdoor games, throw a ball round, play hoop and ball (throw a hoop and someone else try to throw a ball through it when it is in the air); all target games are good like archery for example. At this time of year, as at the others, it is an opportunity to let go of unwanted things in our lives. One way we have marked the season (as yet I've not done this with children but I don't see why one shouldn't) is to light a bonfire and ask the people who will attend to wear or bring something that represents a part of her or himself that s/he wishes to be rid of. They would then at an appropriate moment throw it on the fire, give thanks for the lesson it has taught them and then ask for a blessing on all that they wish for the summer months to come.

> For the May Day is the great day
> Sung along the old great track
> And those who ancient lines did ley
> Will heed this song that calls them back
> Ian Anderson

Goddess for Beltaine

Demeter

Demeter, whose origins are Cretan, is one of my favourite Goddesses. Demeter's long hair is ripe and golden as the summer corn. She has wide shoulders and broad hips and her eyes sparkle with the bright sunlight of constant summer. She has many, many beautiful children.

Demeter is the Greek for Ker – one of the earliest names for the Great Mother and the Grain Goddess. She is the Goddess of summer and the Triple Grain Goddess. The Maiden of the Wheatfield is still seen in the English/Scottish Border custom of making a 'kern-baby'. The last few gleanings of corn from the last field of the harvest are bound together to make a Corn maiden. At the end of the harvest she follows the last of the carts home, carrying the moon-sickle and sheaves in her arms and accompanied by reapers and music. The practice of making Corn Dollies continues to the present day throughout Britain.

Her beautiful and favourite daughter is Persephone who goes on a journey to the Underworld. Their story is one of a journey from childhood to adulthood and also represents the turning of the seasons. It is often told as Spring is felt in the air. Although Demeter is a Summer goddess, her story with her daughter can be told at any time of the year and is especially poignant when we see new growth all around us in the trees, the flowers and animals.

DEMETER AND PERSEPHONE

Long ago and deep within Demeter the Earth Mother, the Great Goddess, wandered through her beautiful garden. She watched as her children played in the warm sunshine. All was well in her garden. All things grew as they should as day after day of rich, warm sunshine and luscious refreshing rain fed the Earth.

Demeter's hair was as ripe and golden as the corn, swaying over her wide shoulders and broad, smooth hips. In her eyes sparkled the bright sunlight of constant summer and from her breasts flowed the milk of a river of stars from the Milky Way.

Demeter had many, many beautiful children, but her greatest joy was her lovely daughter Persephone, long limbed and agile, hair and eyes as dark and flashing as the night and her heart loving and generous. Persephone loved to play and dance and sing and all who knew her felt happy and light hearted.

One day, when Persephone was out playing in the meadows, she heard a strange sound like voices crying. She wondered what it could be and so she went off to try to find where it was coming from. She searched all over the meadow and into the wood but could not get any nearer to the sound.

As evening drew on, Persephone asked her mother what the strange sound could be but Demeter did not want to worry her daughter and began to talk of other things.

But the crying did not go away and the next day Persephone was again playing in the meadows and again heard the distant crying of voices. She was drawn to the aching sound and this time she discovered a tiny crack in the Earth. She squeezed her slender fingers in and pulled and pulled at the crack until it began to open. Wider and wider it became until Persephone could see deep down into the Earth. And there she saw people who were crying. Here were the souls of the dead, lost in the dark of the Underworld. Persephone was filled with compassion for the weeping souls and pulled at the Earth until the opening was wide enough for her to climb down into the cool darkness. Down and down she went and as she descended the earth silently closed over her head.

That same evening, when Demeter waited for her daughter to return from her play she was nowhere to be found. Demeter was beside herself with worry and searched far and wide to find her. She asked everyone she met if they had seen Persephone but no one could help. At last, tired and afraid, Demeter went to the Sun Goddess, Grainne who, from her great height, looked down and said to Demeter, "Your daughter has entered the Underworld, for there is work she must do. There is nothing you can do here but wait and prepare for her return."

Demeter was far from reassured and went home sadly. She was so sad and depressed because she did not have her beloved daughter by her side that she sat with her far seeing eyes cast downwards and forgot to make things grow.

And slowly the Earth became cold and the sky filled with clouds and the rain fell and then the snow fell and the earth lay silent and still...

Persephone, while her mother waited, went deeper and deeper down through the Earth and as she pushed forward her clothes caught and tore and her beautiful hair tangled and twisted. At last she came to the Great World Tree at the centre of the Underworld where she finally caught and hung upside down and died......

There she hung, as still and quiet as the snow covered Earth above, for three days and three nights. But here she was not alone. She was cared for and coaxed back to life by Hel, her beloved sister-Goddess of the Underworld and wise old Hecate, the Crone.

As Persephone was restored to life so she came to understand the cycle of life and death and life again and was able to lead the lost souls of the dead out of the Underworld and into Life again.

Soon Persephone played again in the meadows and her mother was joyous and the Earth once again became fertile and abundant. But, each year, Persephone hears again the voices of the lost souls, and she goes deep down under the Earth to continue her work and each year the Earth becomes still and cold and rests and waits for spring when Persephone will return.

THINGS TO DO

Time to Play

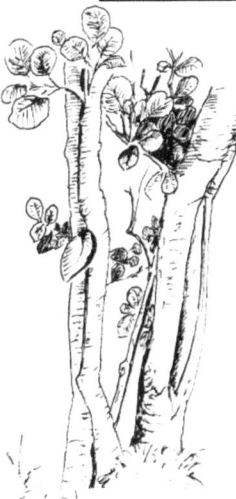

'O do not tell the priest our plight,
For he would call it sin,
For we've been out in the woods all night,
A 'conjuring summer in.
I bring good news by word of mouth,
Good news for cattle and corn,
For now is the sun come out of the South,
With Oak, and Ash, and Thorn.'
Rudyard Kipling

There is no one time to suggest that we go outside and make the most of nature but Beltaine is such an inspirational time that it is good to encourage it, if it is not already happening. At this time of year trees have got their 'see through' leaves and it is a wonderful time to go out and lie down under a tree and look up through the leaves – particularly Alder and Birch with their finely shaped leaves. My friend Jenny, who does a lot of outdoor work with young people, loves this time of year and says it is the only time when you can see both worlds of summer and winter – the bare trees of winter starting to shoot their new buds and leaves of summer. She likes to encourage people to look at beauty, the Beauty of Mother Earth that is all around us.

When encouraging children and indeed anyone to appreciate nature try to forget about 'teaching' and aim to share. Tell them about your feelings about the things they are seeing. I love Rowan or Mountain Ash trees, my birth tree, not just because they are beautiful but because they have a fascinating folklore about them and because I have seen them growing in the most unlikely places and seen how they seem to survive no matter what the circumstances and surroundings. I remember one that was hanging on to what looked like bare rock with its 'toes' and still seemed to be alive. It was growing at a 90º angle from the rock and looked like a weeping tree. My enthusiasm for this tree sparked off an interest in those with whom I shared it. Children respond much more freely to observations than to textbook explanations.

Remember when you are outdoors with children it often brings out a natural spontaneous enthusiasm. Be ready to respond to it, listening to what they are saying and asking. I have had some of my most in-depth and interesting conversations with children I have worked with when we were out walking together.

When you are outdoors something exciting or interesting is always happening. Be ready to respond.

Outdoor plays about the battle between light and dark are good fun at this time of year if you have somewhere to perform them.

Also remember to stay up all night on Beltaine eve. Going 'A Maying' was the custom of going out all night to hunt through the woods for the first branches of flowering hawthorn, and bring them back to deck the houses on the one day when this plant is allowed in the home.

May Queen and King

You may like to choose a May Queen and her consort for your celebrations. They can be adults or children. You can then go carolling from door to door to call folk to join your festivities.

Come join with us, May-pluckers all,
For thus we do begin-O,
To lead our lives to summer-time
Or else it comes not in-O!

Chorus

With two and fro, sing merry-O!
With two and fro sing merry!
With two and fro sing merry-O!
With two and fro sing merry!

We have been rambling half the night
And dangling half the morn-O
And now we're rantling back again
To bear the flowers and thorn-O

Chorus

We have been rambling half the night
And dangling half the morn-O
And now we're rantling back again
To bear the flowers and thorn-O

Chorus

O we were up before the day
To fetch the summer home –O
Now summer we have brought it home,
And winter's made 'is moan-O

Chorus

Then let us all most merry be
And sing with lusty voice-O
And we will have a chance or two
This morning to rejoice-O

Chorus

St George shall next be in our song,
St George he is our knight-O
Of all the knights in all the year
This knight is always upright-O

Chorus

St George send now his right and might,
St George send power to upstand-O
May maids bloom white by day and night,
St George for merry England-O

Chorus

Norman Isles

Merry, as in Merry or even Merrie England relates to Fairy, and it was a time when the magic of the Fairy Queen, the White Lady, was to be seen across the land.

Goose Grass Crowns

We love making these. Pick a large bunch of goose grass and twist it round into a garland to wear on your head. They can be easily twisted round so that they stay in place. We try not to pick wild flowers so you may like to add small decorations of anything that has fallen, like feathers, leaves etc.

Still Hunting

Go outside and find a quiet spot. Stay very still and see what wild life you can see or that comes to you. You will have to make sure that you are not standing, sitting or lying near to anyone else. You will be amazed what wonders you will see.

Blind Walk

In pairs, one person is blindfolded while the other leads. The leader takes her partner for a guided walk through the forest / wood / glade / field / garden or wherever you are. Let him experience the sounds, smells and feel of his surroundings.

This idea can be extended to introducing your partner to a tree. Ask him to see if he can put his arms around it...are there plants around it?...what is the bark like?...Let your partner get to know his tree and then lead him away from it. Remove the blindfold and let the person try to find his tree.

Lie Back And Listen

Get a group to lie in a circle on their backs and hold their fists up in the air. With eyes open or closed, depending what you are asking them to observe, every time someone hears a new bird song, sound or animal sound, or sees a colour bird or animal, she lifts a finger.

See if you can count to ten without hearing a birdsong.

Trails

A Treasure Trail takes some preparing but is very rewarding and great fun. This can be done on bikes or on foot. Have clues placed in various places around a chosen area. The area can range from someone's garden to a whole village. If you are happy to use cars and you have enough adults taking part then you can go even further. With cars you may need to give each person taking part a sheet with all the clues on at the beginning but for individual players on foot you can place the clues at each stop. My father was

very good at this and made each clue a little rhyme.

This can be extended to a Nature Trail where the group are led to look at certain things about them on a trail or an Un-nature Trail.
This needs to be well prepared beforehand. Place along a trail 10 to 15 person-made objects. Some of them can be well disguised and some can be more obvious and blend with their surroundings. Don't tell the group how many things there are. Let the group walk around the trail one at a time with intervals between them trying to spot (but not pick up) as many objects as they can. When they reach the end of the trail let them whisper in your ear how many they saw. If no one saw all of them, tell everyone how many were seen but that there are still more. Let them start again. This can lead on to some excellent discussions about camouflage.

What Am I?

On a piece of paper write the name of an animal, insect, flower or tree, and then stick one onto the back of each person. The person has to go around asking other members of the group questions. The other members may only answer 'yes' or 'no' to the questions. Once they have all found out what they are and if you have used things from the surrounding area, they can go and see if they can find one. Try not to disturb the insect, animal or plant.

Colour Aware

Ask the group or person to look for as many blue things as he can find, then red, then yellow etc. Then look for specific things such as plants or insects, and see how many colours you can see on them.

Hat Walk

You need a large 'hat' – a clean dustbin lid does very well. In pairs put the lid on your head and see how far you can go. Don't hold on to the hat.

It helps if the walkers are the same size and don't get the giggles, and can avoid the temptation of holding or adjusting the lid . . . and walk in the same direction.

Simple Tissue Paper Flowers

You will need

- circles of tissue paper in different colours
- fine wire or strong grass stems
- sticky tape

Fold the tissue circle in half without scoring the paper and then in half again.

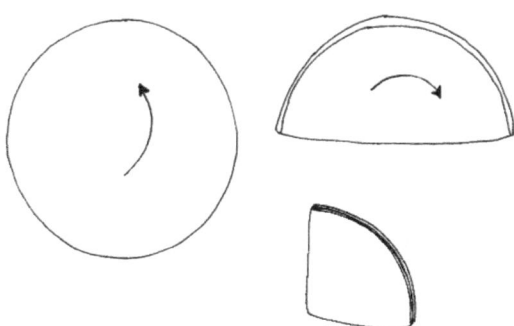

Twist the paper at the tip of the triangle.

Push the wire or grass through the centre, twist the end and secure with the sticky tape.

Tissue Paper Peonies.

You will need

- 2 sheets of tissue paper in different shades.
- florist's wire
- green plastic covered wire
- green crêpe paper (optional)
- quick drying glue

Each sheet of tissue paper measures about 50cms x 74cms (20" x 30"). Divide each sheet into six equal squares by folding the paper in half and then into three. For each flower you will need three squares of one shade for the centre petals and three squares of the other colour for the outer petals.

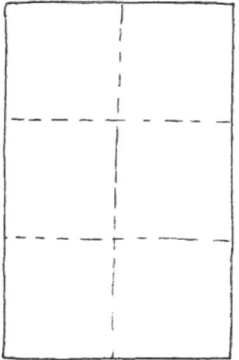

(one sheet of tissue paper folded into 6 squares)

Take a tissue square and fold it in half, in half again, and in half once more, making the creases as sharply as possible, (figs a - d).

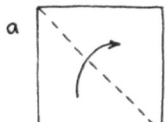 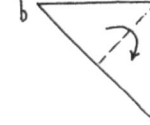  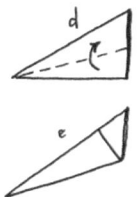

Finally fold the triangle into an irregular cone shape as shown in figure e)

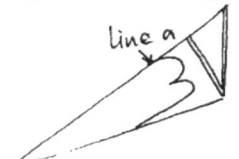 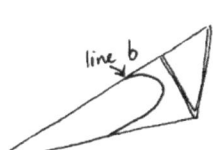

To make the shape of the petals cut line **a** for the inner petals and line **b** for the outside petals. Cut three of each.

Spread out the petals but do not flatten them. Dab a spot of glue onto the centre of each of the petals and place them one on top of the other, taking care to keep the creases in.

Take a stem wire and bend the top over to prevent the petals from falling off. Push the wire through the centre of all six layers of petals. Push the centre of the petals close to the wire so that a 'trumpet' shape is formed. Hold it in place until the glue begins to hold. Secure the base of the flower by binding tightly with the florist's wire or green plastic-covered wire.

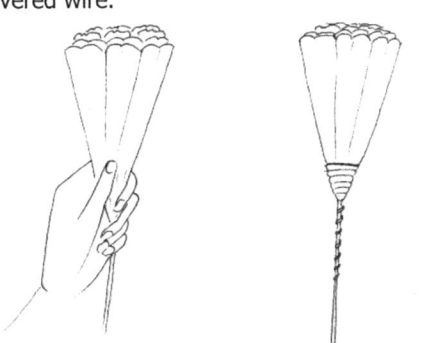

Shape the flower gently separating each of the layers of the outer petals and turning them downwards, and by separating the inner petals and leaving them standing vertically.

If you want to you can cover the wire stem with green crepe paper by wrapping a 2.5cms (1") strip all the way down the stem and securing both ends with glue.

Marigold Wreath

You will need

- hoop of rowan or willow branches
- marigolds
- wire
- gold and silver thread
- gold and silver glass balls

Carefully bend the rowan branches into an oval, binding them with wire as you go.

Work until you have a firm base of branches that can hold it's shape. (If you prefer you can work with a ready-made wreath base from a florist or craft shop.)

Bind in the marigolds around the wreath at intervals.

Hang the gold and silver balls in the centre to represent the Sun and Moon. Alternately you can make a sun and moon shape from card or papier-mâché (see page 34 Papier-mâché, method two, Cut Out Shapes) and paint or spray them gold and silver.

May Day Baskets

A favourite May Day activity is that of making woven baskets overflowing with flowers, sweets and poems, which are left anonymously at homes to bring joy to the finder. The basket is simple to make, woven out of strips of paper.

You will need

- -strips of paper 21cms x 28cms (8½" x 11")(actually any size will do depending on what size you want the end result!)
- - sticky tape or glue

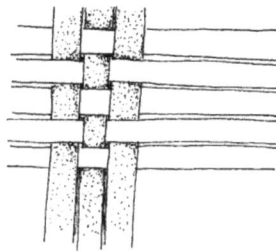

Weave a sheet out of your strips of paper. Twist the sheet round to form a cone and secure the ends tightly.

Fill your May basket with whatever gifts you want and give it with love and bright blessings.

Simple Ritual Gown

This is a very simple design taken from a gown brought back from Ghana. The size will need to be worked out by measuring yourself (or whoever you are making it for) from wrist to wrist when arms are held out to the side and from neck to floor.

You will need
- - material (enough to cover double the appropriate area when measured)
- - thread for sewing up
- - thread for decoration

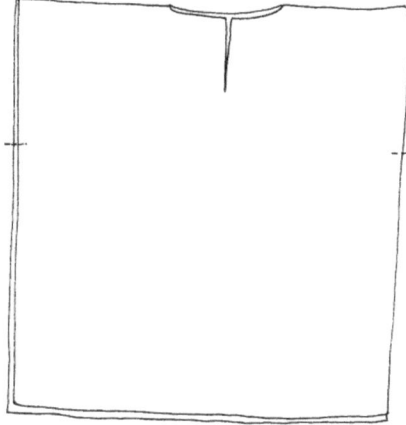

Fold the material as shown in diagram. Cut away a piece for the head (mine is 20cms / 8" wide) and slit down at the front as far as desired. Hem the neck. (You may prefer to cut out a curved neckline.)

Sew the edges up to the desired sleeve opening (Mine leaves a 38cms /15" sleeve opening). Hem the edges of the sleeves and the bottom edge. If you are using a material that doesn't fray then the design is even simpler as you will not need to hem it.)

Decorate around the neck as desired. Mine is tie-dyed in white and purple.

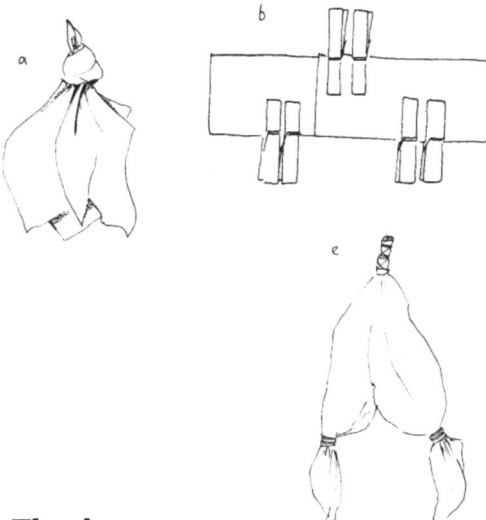

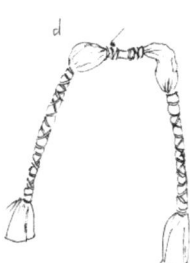

Tie-dye

Tie-dyeing is a way of decorating cloth by blocking out certain parts so that they do not 'take' the dye in which the cloth is dipped. This is done by knotting, folding, clipping, tying or binding the cloth so that the dye cannot penetrate these areas.

Any material that is receptive to dye can be used, cotton and silk being particularly good.

You will need
- material clean, dry and free from creases

- cold water dyes (there is now a great variety of dyes including ones that can be used in a microwave oven
- string (fishing line, plastic cord, rope and linen thread can be used. Cotton thread is not so good as it lets the colour through.)
- dye bath (old bowl, pan etc.)
- scissors

Tie your material in any way you like. See diagrams for ideas. You can use anything to bind the material – paper clips, clothes pegs, bulldog clips, pipe cleaners; anything that grips the fabric, keeps dyes out and is not itself harmed in the dyebath (remembering not to use metal if you are dying the material in a microwave oven).

When your ties are all securely tied, wet the cloth thoroughly and put it into the dyebath for the length of time stated in the manufacturer's instructions.

When the dye has taken, remove the fabric, leaving the ties intact, and rinse it thoroughly. Do not undo the ties until the cloth has had time to dry or dye may seep into the white, unprotected areas.

When undoing the ties it is very easy to nip the cloth accidentally so be sure to insert the point of the scissors under the end, not the middle of the tie.

For special effects you can use bleach to remove colour from areas that have been dyed. Make sure the bleach will not 'burn' the material. Or add the material, a part at a time, so that some areas are in the dye longer than others and will have a deeper colour. I did this with a muslin curtain that I was making for a friend's bathroom and the result looked like water at different depths. (I stamped gold stars onto the finished curtain.)

Alder Cone Bees

These are very easy to make and look delightful hanging in the window or over a flower arrangement.

You will need
- dried alder cones
- yellow wool (fluffy if possible)
- white tissue paper
- white cotton thread
- scissors

Wrap a little piece of the yellow wool around an alder cone so that the cone looks like the body of a bee. Snip the end of the wool at the required length and tuck the two ends in to the cone.

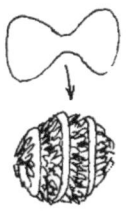

Cut out a simple wing shape like a figure of eight from the tissue paper and press it into the alder cone.

Attach some cotton to hang the bee up. I have made several bees and hung them from a little willow circle (about 8 cm / 3" in diameter), which makes a very attractive mobile.

Chilled Tomato Soup

This is a wonderful recipe for those warm days that are coming.

You will need

- 450g/1 lb tomatoes, skinned
- 110g/4 ozs cucumber, skinned
- 1 clove garlic
- 2 teaspoons Tamari sauce
- 1 green pepper, deseeded and chopped
- 150g/5ozs carton yoghurt

Put aside ½ the pepper and the yoghurt. Liquidise the rest and then stir in the yoghurt and rest of the pepper. Chill before serving.

Mushroom Flower cups

This is a lovely, summery recipe, which I have used as a starter or a main dish.

8 – 12 large mushrooms
¼ cup ground almonds
3 tablespoons yoghurt
squeeze lemon juice
fresh parsley
vegetable bouillon powder to taste

Remove the stalks of the mushrooms and chop them finely. Mix with the ground almonds and then add the yoghurt and lemon juice. Add the parsley and bouillon powder. Pour the mixture into the upturned mushrooms and garnish with fresh mint or parsley.

Song for Imbolc
Deep Within My Heart

H.Royall

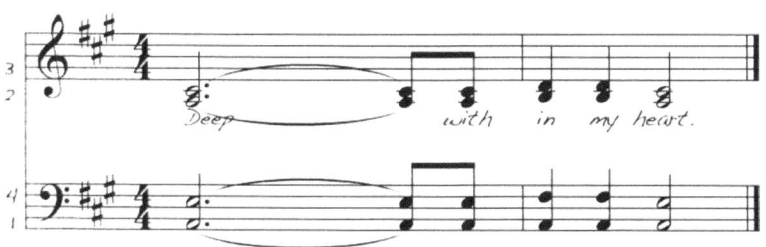

Sing this on its own or as an accompaniment to the following tune.
It sounds good when you build it up bringing one line in at a time in
the order shown.

THE STAR

Twinkle, twinkle little star.
How I wonder what you are!
Up above the world so high,
Like a diamond in the sky.

When the blazing sun is gone,
When she nothing shines upon,
Then you show your little light,
Twinkle, twinkle all the night.

Then the traveller in the dark,
Thanks you for your tiny spark,
He could not see which way to go,
If you did not twinkle so.

In the dark blue sky you keep,
And often through my windows peep.
For you never shut your eye,
'Till the sun is in the sky.

As your bright and tiny spark,
Lights the traveller in the dark,
Though I know not what you are,
Twinkle, twinkle little star.

Jane Taylor

Summer Solstice

Celebration Time

SUMMER SOLSTICE AND MIDSUMMER DAY or LITHA
(21st June & 24th June)

In farming communities the summer was a time of hard work and toil to reap the benefits of the growing season. Long hours of work would be needed to weed and hoe all the crops. The sheep would have been sheared and the women would be busy spinning the wool. In England, after sundown, large bonfires would be lit on Midsummer Eve, which would provide light to the revellers and ward off evil spirits. Similar to the traditions at Beltaine people often jumped through the fires for good luck. In addition to these fires, the streets were lined with lanterns, and the people carried their own little lanterns as they wandered from one bonfire to another. Lighting the bonfires was known as 'setting the watch' while the wandering bands were called a 'marching watch'. Often Morris dancers and other traditional players joined them.

The summer solstice is the high point of the sun when he is at his strongest, but it is also the day when he begins to weaken. Once again the year has turned and the great wheel goes on. The Druids would worship in their oak groves and the Old Ones would meet at the ancient monument at Avebury, in Wiltshire, the great sun temple of old.

At dawn the sun can be greeted from a hill facing east. Now the best of the summer will follow and we ask that the sun will bless the crops and give us a good harvest.

Summer Solstice was another excuse to deck the halls (although mainly over the front doors) with boughs of greenery. Five plants were thought to have special magical properties on this night: rue, roses, St. John's wort, vervain and trefoil.

This was an important time for the faery folk who especially liked to go a riddling. Remember to wear your jacket inside out if you venture out on this fine summer night. If you get lost seek out one of the 'ley lines', the old straight tracks, until you get home. This will keep you safe, as will crossing a stream of living (running) water.

Puck.	How now, spirit! whither wander you?
Fairy.	Over hill over dale,
	Through bush, through briar,
	Over park, over pale,
	Through flood, through fire,
	I do wander every where,
	Swifter than the moonës sphere:
	And I serve the Fairy Queen,
	To dew her orbs upon the green.
	The cowslips tall her pensioners be,
	In their gold coats spots you see:
	Those be rubies, fairy favours:
	In those freckles live their savours.
	I must go seek some dewdrops here,
	And hang a pearl in every cowslip's ear.
	Farewell, thou lob of spirits: I'll be gone-
	Our queen and all her elves come here anon.

'A Midsummer Night's Dream'
from 'The Complete Works of Shakespeare' Cambridge University Press

This is the time of year to be out of doors, enjoying the sunshine (if it's not a cold summer), the time for barbecues and beach parties. My friend Ruth celebrates this time of year by inviting friends round to a garden party. They have a beautiful garden and place the food that she has prepared and the contributions from friends onto outdoor tables. Each year the guests try to outdo each other with sumptuous puddings and sweets. She prepares a Pimms cocktail in a large glass bowl and a fruit cocktail for those who don't want alcohol. The tables overflow with strawberries and cream, salads and fresh fruit. The children all meet up and play together in the sunshine and as Ruth is lucky enough to live near a beach they can enjoy the beauty of a walk by the sea and give thanks for the energy and warmth of the sun and the power and life force of the water.

Goddess for Summer Solstice

Grainne

In Scottish and Irish Gaelic, Greine or Grian is a feminine word meaning the Sun. In her book 'The Ancient British Goddess' Kathy Jones says, "From all the indications in the earliest languages of the British Isles the Sun was known as the Mother of All Life on Earth. In the daytime she gave her light and heat to the world. At sunset she descended beneath the sea or into the waters of the earth through wells or ponds to regenerate the world. In the summertime she blessed the earth with her fiery energy and brought all plants and grain to fruition."

In the Irish legend of The Romance of Grainne and Diarmid, the Sun Goddess Grainne compels her lover Diarmid to follow her, while her husband pursues them for 'a year and a day'. This is the story of the making of the solar year of 365 days formed from thirteen lunar months of 28 days plus one more day.

Grainne is the bright, shining gold and yellow of the sun. Her symbols are gold and yellow, a gold disc, or any other symbol that could represent the sun, and ripe golden grain.

THE OLD APPLE TREE

Long ago, not far from the edge of a wood there stood an old, old tree. It was hard to know what sort of tree it was. Its branches were knotted and bent and it bore few leaves and neither fruit nor flowers.

One day a young boy came to the edge of the wood where the tree grew. He was angry. He was often angry these days though he was not sure why. This particular day he was determined to stay out all night and show that he wasn't afraid of the dark, in fact he wasn't afraid of anything thank you very much! His mother would worry but what did he care; she was always worrying. And as for his friends, they were always egging him on to do stupid things to prove himself, things they wouldn't do themselves, oh no! The more he thought about it the more angry he became and he swung his overnight bag over his shoulder, took a firmer grip on his axe and stomped on looking for a likely place to camp.

At last he stopped by the old tree and threw his bag down. 'This looks perfect', he thought, 'I can cut some of this old tree to light a fire and make a nice cosy bed on this moss here.' Gripping his axe the boy swung it back to strike at a branch of the tree but the old tree shuddered and the boy's swing went wide. He let his axe arm fall and stared at the tree.

Then he pulled himself together. 'I'm not afraid of a stupid old tree, I'm not afraid of the wood, I'm not afraid of the dark!' and feeling more angry than ever he swung his axe to try again. This time the tree shuddered even harder and let out a low moan.

At this the boy dropped his axe and ran a little away from the tree. His heart was beating fast and his knees were beginning to give way. 'This is ridiculous' he thought, 'only kids are afraid of the wood and I'm a man. There's nothing there so I'll just go back and make a comfortable bed for the night and maybe I won't cut the branches of that tree until later when I need the fire.'
He went back to his bedroll and sat under the tree and looked out over the view of the hills on that beautiful summer evening, as the sun turned the clouds salmon pink and gold and the cows moved lazily in the distance. Soon the boy began to doze and from deep in his dream a voice seemed to speak to him. Old, so old the voice seemed, as if it were as bent and twisted as the old tree he leant against.

'Is it courage you seek' creaked the voice, 'the courage of eagles and of mountains?' and as she spoke a picture of a young apple tree drifted into his mind and he saw her standing bare and cold in the frozen winter.
'Where are your leaves? How will you survive the cold?' he asked. The apple tree replied, 'It is the way I understand the winter, the way I learn courage and strength.'
'What is courageous about standing out in the cold where you could die?' The apple tree laughed and between her branches the boy saw a picture of himself in the playground at school. The group of boys with him were laughing and encouraging him to join them in spoiling the younger boys' game of football, but he refused.
'Sometimes it takes great courage to stand alone.' said the old tree. 'Courage comes from deep within, the courage to stand out in the cold.' and the picture faded from his mind and was replaced by spring.

Now the apple tree was covered in delicate pink and white blossoms. The boy thought she looked beautiful and then he pulled himself together. 'Look at those petals, they aren't going to last. They're just flimsy and useless.' he said crossly as a waft of sweet fragrance filled his nostrils.

'In spring I choose to welcome all nature with my beautiful flowers. Without my gift of blossoms I would not attract all the wonderful birds and insects and I would not learn the lesson of gratefulness, I am grateful for the gifts of spring.' And as she spoke the boy saw insects on the tree and heard the buzzing of the bees and his mind drifted to his mother. He saw as if he was looking through her eyes at the tree and he knew in that moment that she worried about him because she loved him. He reached out to touch her, to tell her not to worry, but she was gone and the picture had moved on to summer.

The tree had dropped her delicate flowers and stood now with shiny green apples and deep green leaves. As summer drew on, the apples grew into hearty red ones and the tree tended and cared for them feeding them and watching them grow. The boy had become so engrossed in watching that he was taken by surprise when a group of children and adults came by and started picking the apples. They were laughing and playing around the tree and the apple tree looked on with great delight sharing their pleasure. 'These people are stealing your fruit!' shouted the boy. 'Why do you look so pleased?'
'Summer is my giveaway time. What good would my apples be if I could not give them away?'
'But if you give everything away what good would that do you?'
The tree laughed and said, 'richness is not what you have, it is what you can give away,' and she tossed an apple at the startled boy. This was a hard one for him to understand. 'Summer is a time to learn the lesson of generosity.'

As summer turned to autumn the apple tree swayed and danced in the gentle breezes and laughed as her golden, pink and brown leaves flew about her making a carpet of colour on the ground. Now the boy was sad. He was growing to like the little apple tree and he did not want her to lose all her wonderful golden leaves.
'Don't be sad,' said the tree, 'autumn is the time for me to learn to have faith. I must let go so that new leaves can grow again and the cycle will be repeated.'

The boy awoke and saw that around where he was sitting there were some old leaves. He jumped up and looked at the tree he had been leaning against. He was a little afraid but he told himself it was a dream, trees don't talk and besides he didn't even know if he had been leaning against an apple tree or not: it was so old and bent that it was unrecognisable.

It was darker now and the boy felt different after his dream, or whatever it was, so he decided he would go home. As he picked up his overnight bag he heard someone approaching. He looked round and saw his younger sister. 'What are you doing out at this time of night?' he asked, too startled to be cross.
'Mind your own business,' she snapped, 'I'm running away. I'm not going back to that stupid school!'
'Why not?'
'My so-called friends are horrible to me, they want to be my best friend one day and they're horrible to me the next and they call me names and it isn't fair! I don't do anything to them, they're just stupid!' and she burst into tears.
'Yeh, it's tough at school sometimes.' said her brother. 'You must feel rotten. Come on, let's go home: you'll be happier there. I'll tell you a story on the way.'
The girl looked up quickly at her brother. She was grateful but a little surprised at his reaction. He smiled. He knew he didn't usually react like this because he was more often than not lost in his own world of problems, but he took her hand and led her along the edge of the wood and on down the hill towards home and as they walked he said, 'once there was an old apple tree………'

With thanks to Sandra Hosler

THINGS TO DO

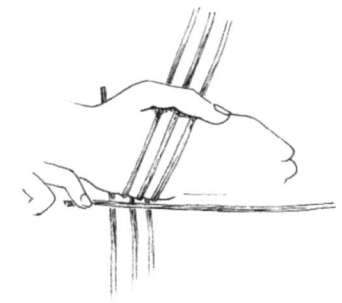

Celebration Time

Hopefully the weather is encouraging everyone to go out of doors and enjoy the sunshine. If you can get to a sandy beach use coloured sand to make a solar mandala. (We try not to encourage people to take sand or pebbles away from beaches so it is a good time to make lovely pictures on the beach, which will be washed away eventually.) Use this glorious time of year to take part in simple rituals and meditations in the open air. Play lots of water games and let the children enjoy being wet and dirty!

We enjoy making presents for the fairies at this time of year. Our favourite was to pick the wild strawberries from Jill's garden and leave them in little hand woven baskets.

Grass basket

You will need
- 12 thick stems of grass
- finer grass for weaving
- large darning needle (optional)

Lay six of the thicker stems of grass close together, horizontally in front of you. Hold them on the working surface with your left hand (if right handed) to the left of centre.

Pick up, and hold in your left hand, the first (the one furthest away from you), third and fifth stems.

Lay another stem across the second, fourth and sixth blades close to your left hand so that when the blades in the left hand are returned to their starting position they form the first row of a check weave.

Now pick up the second, fourth and sixth stem. (This is easier if you start picking up the next row while putting down the stems you have just worked – no. 2 up, no. 1 down, no 4 up, no. 3 down etc.) Pull the stems gently as they are put down to keep the check tight.

Continue until all six vertical stems are in place and your check weave centre is complete.

Begin weaving the finer grasses bending one stem, not quite in the middle and loop it around a stake. Weave the grass stem in and out, each end of stem going in the opposite direction from the other. If you are using grass with heads use them to decorate by leaving the heads on the outside of the basket.

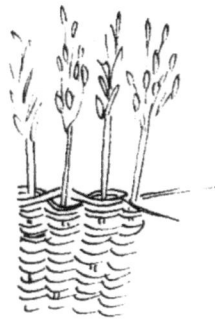

Continue until you have a small basket shape. To finish, sew the end of the weaving stem into the body of the basket with the needle. (If you are in a field, use your fingers or leave the ends on the inside of the basket.) Weave the stakes in the same way to finish the border. Leave ends on the inside.

Grass Dolls

My friend, Rae, had a Croning Party where we celebrated her move from Mother to Crone. She asked us to make a doll out of grass to represent ourselves and then we put them in a ring with hers in the middle to represent her ring of friendship. My daughter really enjoyed this party and has still got a photograph of her grass doll.

You will need
- a large bunch of grasses with their flower heads on
- string to bind (or strong wool)
- scissors

Line up the grass heads and bend as shown.

Insert grass without heads for the arms. Trim and tie.
This is only one way. Experiment and see what you can come up with. In our group we made as many different types of doll as there were people.
These dolls look lovely when they are green and also when they have dried.

Block Printing with Fruit & Vegetables

You will need
- fruit and/or vegetables
- thick, water based paint or fabric dyes for chunky designs
- paintbrush
- paper (not glossy) or material
- vegetable knife
- rags
- old blanket or piece of felt

If working with fabric, place a piece of felt or blanket on a table to give some softness underneath the fabric being printed. Place your fabric on top of this.

Cut fruit or vegetable in half, do not remove any skins as this defines the shape and holds the cut piece together. Dry it gently with a rag.

Apply the paint or dye fairly liberally with the stiff brush to the cut face of the fruit/vegetable and do a test print on a scrap of paper or material. Do not bang the fruit/vegetable down as it may slide around, but carefully place it and apply gentle pressure. Lift the fruit/vegetable away from the paper or fabric very carefully.

Well Dressing

Well dressing has long been a tradition in all parts of England where the wells are blessed and decorated with flower petals, moss and leaves pressed into beds of damp clay. These pictures were fitted into frames around the wells to give thanks for the supply of water. Many of the wells were dedicated to different Goddesses.
Collect some clay and press the damp clay onto a tray. Press petals and leaves and other coloured bits into a pattern or picture.

Leave to dry in the garden. You may like to dedicate your picture to someone or something.

Dried/Pressed Flowers

Fallen flowers can be very beautiful if pressed and made into pictures, cards or decoration. Little elderflower heads look like tiny stars and rose petals are lovely to make into fragrance or to dry and use for confetti or pot-pourri. I dried a bunch of roses that a friend had sent me by hanging them upside down and then using them to make some incense.

Midsummer Incense

You will need
- 2 parts Frankincense (you can buy this resin, usually in small lumps about the size of cat litter)
- 2 parts Rose Petals
- 1 part Vervain
- 1 part Mugwort
- 1 part Lavender flowers

Wash the cuttings of vervain, Mugwort and lavender, so that they are free of dirt and then hang them upside down for a few weeks until dry. Hang the roses or dry the rose petals. Make sure you don't hang them too close together or they will go mouldy. When dry, mix them together, slightly crushed or torn. Keep in an airtight jar and use sparingly. You will need a special incense burner and charcoal. If you enjoy making your own incense you would do well to keep a notebook of ingredients.

Making Scents

Rose Water

You will need
- 1 cup distilled water
- 2½ tablespoons vodka
- ½ cup fresh rose petals
- 10 drops rose fragrance oil

Fill a sterilised glass jar with rose petals and pour water and vodka over the petals, stirring gently with a glass rod or stainless steel spoon. Add the rose oil and seal with an airtight lid. Store in a cool place for one week and stir every few days. Strain the liquid through cheesecloth or a paper filter and discard the petals. Rose water should be bottled immediately in an airtight bottle and can be kept for six to eight months. If making without alcohol use within one month.

You can also make lavender water using the same method using ½ cup of lavender flowers fresh or dried. Lavender water can be stored in a dark bottle and kept for up to one year.

Picnics

Picnics are all the more fun when part of an unexpected outing to make the most of the lovely sunny weather or just because you want to. Get into the habit of saving containers with secure tops to transport dressings etc. Pack food carefully and keep dressing separate from salads. Pack cutlery, tablecloth and table ware last so that they are the first to be taken out. Keep cool bottles in the freezer as soon as the weather turns warm. Take a bin liner for dirty plates and one for rubbish. If using a vacuum flask, fill it right to the top as any air will reduce the flask's insulating properties.

Omelette Rolls

Wafer-thin omelettes make a delicious alternative to sandwiches. Once cool, roll the omelettes up with a savoury filling. Cover tightly and refrigerate until required. Slice thickly to serve.

You will need
- 8 eggs (one egg per omelette)
- seasoning
- butter or oil
- fresh herbs (optional)

Lightly whisk the eggs adding a little milk or water if required. Add seasoning and herbs.

Heat a little butter or oil in a 25.5cm (10") non-stick frying pan. Add a small ladle of the egg mixture and swirl around the pan to give a thin layer. Leave to set and brown for about 30 seconds.
Loosen around the edges and then turn out the omelette onto a sheet of greaseproof paper.
Cook all the omelettes similarly. Stack up with greaseproof paper between each omelette. Cover and cool.
Stuff the omelettes with a delicious savoury filling. My daughter's favourite is mixed salad, chopped into small pieces, and dressing added.

Going Hunting

Send the children (and adults) out for a scavenger hunt. Chose a theme like the four elements – earth, air, fire and water, with the fifth Chinese element (wood) if you like – or a colour or texture or senses. Ask the group to bring back a certain number of objects, or to go for a certain length of time, and then have a gathering time when you look at all the treasures and talk about them (if you want to). It is a good idea to carry a bell or whistle if you are sending a group out and you want to be able to call them back. We have a duck call which is great fun.

Expert Advice

You may know someone in the local community who knows about an aspect of wildlife. See if you can arrange to meet them and find out about their subject. There are all sorts of people who help out in local woods and nature areas. We have spent many happy hours in Monk Wood and Tiddsley Wood going on insect spotting walks, bark rubbing, meeting different animals and enjoying lots of local art and crafts when they have open days.

Charcoal Drawing

If you are making a fire you may be able to use some of the charred wood to do some charcoal drawings. Messy and great fun! Perhaps you could use your drawings to play a game like Give Us An Art Clue. Remember the safety code when using things from a hot fire.

Night Walk

Decide where you are going beforehand and make the whole walk part of the experience. Carry some safe form of lighting but don't let the children use torches so that they get their 'night eyes'. As you are walking to the place you have chosen see how quietly you can move along. You may like to use some well-known character as an example – a Hobbit, an Elf, Robin Hood or an animal. Listen out for sounds, what can you feel, smell, see, hear? . . .
When you arrive at the chosen place sit the group (if there are several participants) in a circle so that they can touch each other. Pass around little film pots (or any little plastic pots with lids). Inside each one have something different and see if they can tell what it is. Lastly pass around a small sheet of paper each and a wax crayon. Ask them

to write the colour of the crayon on the sheet of paper.

Light your lantern or lamp and discuss how you did. Talk about the change in senses in the dark. Talk about fear. If they were not at all frightened there is something wrong. Talk about the advantages of being frightened to some degree. End with a story if you have time and inclination. Ghost or frightening stories are OK but my daughter doesn't like them so I very rarely tell them unless they are funny.

Star Night Walk

You may like to make some constellation cards. Draw one constellation on each card and on the back the name and some information about it. Give each person a card and see if they can spot their constellation. Or you may want to get a star map or take someone who knows the constellations and can tell you about them.

Ratatouille

This is the only version of this dish that I have really enjoyed. It has now become one of our regular summer dishes.

1 aubergine
1 medium or large onion
2 cloves garlic
1 tablespoon olive oil
1 tablespoon fresh basil
450g/1 lb fresh skinned tomatoes
1 green pepper, deseeded, chopped
175g/6ozs fresh mushrooms
225g/8ozs courgettes, chopped
1 tablespoon vegetable bouillon powder
3 tablespoons chopped fresh parsley

Cut the aubergine into 10cm (½") cubes and chop the onion into fairly large pieces. Chop the garlic finely. Heat the oil, then brown the aubergine, onion and garlic in the oil for 5 – 10 minutes. Add the basil and cook for one more minute. Add the tomatoes, pepper, mushrooms, courgettes and bouillon powder and simmer for about 25 minutes or until the vegetables are how you like them. Season and sprinkle with parsley. May be served hot or cold.

Summer Dressing

This is the dressing I use throughout summer and beyond, which I put on dishes such as salads, jacket potatoes, steamed vegetables.

3 cups olive oil (or sunflower if you prefer)
1 cup cider vinegar
1 tomato skinned
1 clove garlic
½ teaspoon mustard
1 teaspoon vegetable Bouillon powder
  mixed herbs – fresh if you have them

Liquidise all the ingredients and store in a cool place.

Banana Bread

This is a lovely way to use up any bananas that have become too ripe. Sometimes we make this and just leave some on the table to offer to any friends who might drop in.

225g/8ozs flour
1½ teaspoons baking powder
½ teaspoon ground ginger
pinch allspice
125g/4ozs sugar
2 tablespoons ground almonds
125g/4ozs melted butter
3 eggs, beaten
rind of one lemon
4 ripe bananas

Grease a loaf tin. Mix together the dry ingredients. Mix the butter, eggs and lemon rind and stir them into the dry ingredients. Beat in the bananas
Cook on Gas mark 4/350F/180C for approximately 1 hour. (Cooking times vary depending on the flour used, I often have to cook for longer than one hour when using wheat free flour.)

Song for Summer Solstice

Grainne, Grainne Mother Sun

H.Royall

Grainne, Grainne, moth-er sun, Shine on the corn and ri-pen the har—vest,

Grainne, Grainne, moth-er sun, Shine, oh shine on me.

Lammas
Gathering Time

LAMMAS - LUGHNASAD
(Pronounced Lunassa)
(1st – 2nd August)

Lammas is the feast and celebration of the fruits and harvest of the life force. We greet Lammas with a mixture of sadness and thanksgiving as we celebrate the harvest of our work through the year and we recognise the solemnity of the death of John Barleycorn, the Lord of the Sun who, having given us his strength, is now cut down.

August would have been a time of harvesting barley oats and wheat. Lammas derives its name from the Old English "Hlafmas" or "loaf-mass" or in Scotland, Lughnasad, the Feast of the Celtic Sun God, Lugh who was the spirit of the growing corn. In Britain this was a time when as many people as possible were brought from their normal work and children from their schools to help with the harvesting. Today the holiday remains as Bank Holiday Monday. The last sheaf of corn would be woven into a Corn Dolly. This would be kept at home on the hearth or alter until next spring when the seeds would be sown again. The harvest season was, and to some extent still is, the most critical of the year.

This was also the traditional time of year for craft festivals. The medieval guilds would create elaborate displays of their wares, decorating their shops and themselves in bright colours and ribbons, marching in parades, and performing strange, ceremonial plays and dances for the entranced onlookers.

Lammas is also the feast of the first fruits. Depending on when the 'first fruits' are for you, celebrate this season with gathering them in.

As we don't have a garden with our own crops to harvest my daughter and I often chose this time of year to go to 'Pick-Your-Own' farms and gather lots of luscious fruit and vegetables to eat raw, cook or preserve. We try out different recipes for bread and once made a large wheat sheaf shaped loaf for our local Unitarian group (a religious group which draws inspiration from many faiths). As both of us are allergic to wheat, coming up with good, wheat free recipes is not always easy but we have discovered some that make the results edible!

The sun is high, the days are long and hot (if we're lucky in England), the wheat is golden and ready to be cut and we sit within our harvest reflecting on all that we have done and all that has grown as a result. It is a good time to reflect on what is good in our lives and celebrate those things. It is a good time to invite friends round and share wonderful, seasonal meals with all the glorious vegetables and fruits that are available at this time of year.

With the development of modern farming methods it is hard to imagine the reapers in the field, all in a line under a warm sky but maybe we can look at the rhythm in our lives and enjoy the natural cycle that produces such a harvest.

O three men they did come down from Kent
To plough for wheat and rye
And they made a vow and a solemn vow
John Barleycorn should die

111

O they ploughed in the furrow deep
Till the clods lay o'er his head
And these three men were rejoicing then
John Barleycorn was dead

They left him there for a week or so
And a shower of rain did fall
John Barleycorn sprung up again
And he proved them liars all

Then they hired men with sickles
To cut him off at the knee
And the worst of all they served Barleycorn
They served him barbarously

Then they hired men with pitchforks
To pitch him onto the load
And the worst of all they served Barleycorn
They bound him down with cord

Then they hired men with thrashels
To beat him high and low
They came smick-smack on poor Jack's back
Till the flesh bled every blow

O the next they put him in the maltin' kiln
Thinking to dry his bones
And the worst of all they served barleycorn
They crushed him between two stones

Then they put him into the mashing tub
Thinking to scald his tail
And the next thing they called Barleycorn
They called him home-brewed ale

So come put your wine into glasses
Your cider in tin-cans
But young Barleycorn in the old brown jug
For he proves the strongest man.

Goddess for Lammas

Pandora

Pandora, the second Goddess, arose from the earth. Mighty and magnificent, she is as earthy as the very Earth herself and surrounded by a glowing halo of golden light. Pandora is the Giver of all Gifts ('pan' meaning all and 'dora' meaning to give). After the world had been created Pandora came to teach people about community, creativity and caring. She pours out her bounty from her large earthenware jar and inundates the land with her grace and abundance.

Pandora stands at the end of summer and the beginning of harvest when the earth gives forth its bounty and recalls her abundance. Her symbols are a cornucopia, an earthenware jar or pot with fruit, such as bright red berries and pomegranate, or gifts spilling out of it.

PANDORA

Long ago and deep within when The Great Mother wove her threads of Life, intricate and beautiful, and the Earth became. Her children walked on the Earth and were unsure of themselves but curious. They searched for food and hid in the undergrowth and besides rocks and rivers.

All that Great Mother had made was beautiful but her children were not really aware of this and spent their time doing no more than eating and hiding, and soon they discovered that there were many things they may have wanted.

One morning, as the sun rose high in a clear arching sky and stretched out with the joy of waking, a fat, young bear bundled over to a hillside where delicious red berries hung heavily from the bushes.

The humans followed with great interest and began to feast on the wonderful food, and were so intent on what they were doing that they did not feel the ground begin to rumble. At first like the gentle heart beat of the living Earth and then louder and louder until the ground at the foot of the hill split open with a mighty crack!

From it arose the Goddess Pandora.

She was mighty and magnificent, and earthy as the very Earth herself. She was surrounded by a glowing halo of golden light and she carried a large earthen jar on her shoulder. She looked down at the terrified people.

Then she smiled and said, "I am Pandora, Giver of All Gifts" and her deep voice flowed in rich cadencies like milk and honey and calmed the people.

She moved to the hillside and sat down and took the lid from her jar. As she reached in, her hand seemed to pass through many colours and she pulled out a pomegranate, which became a pear, which became a lemon, which became a fig.

"I bring you fruit trees which will bear fruit to fill you and satisfy your hunger, and this my generous grapevine that will always give you enough to drink."

Then she reached into the jar again with her beautiful, fat hand and scooped out a handful of seeds and scattered them over the hillside.

"There, see now, you will have herbs and flowers for eating and healing, for weaving and dying, and beneath my surface you will find ore and mineral and clay. But do not value one gift over another and tend each one well." And as she spoke she took two flat stones and struck them together until sparks seemed to fly from her hands and she said, "Here is flint".

The people stared at her in wonder as they stood near, bathed in her aura and watched as she pushed the pitcher onto its side, inundating the hillside with her flowing grace, and filling the valley with rainbow light.

All the great gifts of Pandora flowed from her pitcher – gifts of understanding and compassion, patience and perception, gifts of wonder and imagination, creativity and community, hope and anger and courage and peace.

As the gifts flowed Pandora stretched out her arms and laughed and said, "I give you the gift of laughter and joy and loving kindness." And her laughter filled the hillside and the valley and rolled across the whole Earth.

THINGS TO DO

Gathering Time

Lammas or Lughnasad is the gathering time, when we begin to appreciate our harvest. It is a time to gather the fruits and vegetables that we have grown and to gather the fruits of our work and thoughts as well.

The end of summer is a lovely time to get out as much as possible. Find places to jump over streams and build dams to collect water. Make outdoor dens and look at the glory of nature all around that can give you ideas of what to do if going for a walk isn't enough. Find a Pick-Your-Own farm and stock up on fruits and vegetables. Now is a good time to start preserving them for the colder season. If you can, collect fruit and dry them for your gingerbread house in Winter Solstice or you can use them for decorations. We always like to have a pile of fruits around a large candle at this time of year to mark the harvest feel to the season.

When a friend of mine's father died she let her children write blessings on balloons and send them up to him. Now would be a lovely time to write a blessing for the world or for someone you know, and send it up on a brightly coloured balloon. Of course this is the sort of activity that you can do at any time of year but I rather like the idea of blessings at Lammas time.

Lammas Pictures

Although the weather may not have started to turn colder and the first misty autumn feeling may not be in the air, as time goes on the leaves will start to turn colour and there will be evidence of dried and beautiful wild growth around. As the season moves on and if you are very careful to choose things that will not be hurt, like nuts and leaves that have already fallen and grasses that have died, you can gather material to make into beautiful Lammas collages. Include leaf prints and natural berry dyes. (Wash your hands as you go along with these, as the fruit will stain.) In our small school one week Ruth, one of the mums, came in with Loganberries and lots of tissue paper from a resource centre and some dried leaves. The children had great fun crushing the berries in the paper, pressing the leaves onto the berry juice and then making leaf prints from them.

You can also add leaf and plant rubbings. Place a leaf under a piece of plain paper and gently rub a wax crayon on its side over the top of the paper.

We are very lucky in our local shops and see some beautiful window arrangements that match the seasons. The children's bookshop had some lovely leaf prints, which had been cut out and mounted on brown and gold sugar paper, which itself was cut to the leaf shape leaving a little border.

Smudge Stick

You will need
- long cuttings of mint, basil, rosemary, lavender, sage
- cotton thread

Wash the cuttings so that they are free of dirt and then hang them upside down for a few weeks until dry. Make sure you don't hang too many together or they will go mouldy.
Bundle a mixture of the herbs together and tie securely with the cotton thread. Light the end of the smudge stick and let it go out leaving just the ends glowing. This can be used instead of the Beltaine fire for cleansing.

Corn Dolls

Corn dollies have been found in various forms all over the world. In England different parts of the country made different types, which have become traditional.
The straw most commonly used is wheat but any hollow centred straw will do including oats, rye and maize. Cut the straw when it is nearly ripe. Dry it by spreading it out to dry in the sun or hang bundles in a dry place like an airing cupboard or a slow oven with the door open. Once dry, straws can be stored for years.
Once the straw has been dried it will split when plaited. To prevent this the straw must be soaked in water. Test by pinching it. If it does not split it is ready. Do not over soak as it becomes too soft to handle with ease. Warm water will speed up the damping process. Do not let the ears get wet. Arrange a damp towel around the straws while you are working – this prevents it from drying before you are ready to use it. If you are unable to obtain corn you can use paper straws.

Five Straw Favour

These were often made by farm hands as love tokens.

You will need
- five straws with ears
- sharp scissors
- raffia

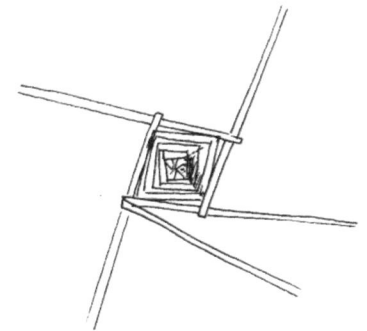

Tie the five straws together just below the ears. With the ears dangling from the weave, spread out the straws so that they make a square. Three corners have one straw each and the fourth has two, which will be the nearest to you. Bend straw A and lay it anti-clockwise over the next two straws close to the centre.
Move the work clockwise so that the last straw you went over (C) is nearest to you.
Take straw C up and over straws A and D keeping it near the centre.
Continue like this always taking the last straw you passed over and moving it anti-clockwise over the next two straws to produce a spiral.

Do not increase the size of the work: keep it constant along its length.
Leave a short length of unwoven straw at the end.

Tie the straws where the weaving ends with the raffia.

Bend the plait into a loop and tie together above the ears.
Trim off excess straw and decorate with a ribbon bow.

Festival Bread

Festival breads have been made for centuries to celebrate abundant harvests. The design of the loaf was determined by the nature of the community. The wheatsheaf form originated in arable farming communities.

The warmth of the kitchen, the creative, hands on quality of the process, finished by fire, makes baking special and sacred.

As we are allergic to wheat we have experimented with various shapes and recipes and have made all sorts of festival bread. The following wheatsheaf was used one year for harvest festival in our local Unitarian Church. It was enjoyed by everyone after the service with a hot vegetable soup. This is a traditional recipe.

1.4 kg (3 lbs 2 ozs) bread flour (I use whole brown but white is better for making an authentic golden design)
25g (1oz) salt

25g (1oz) fat (preferably lard if you are not vegetarian)
25g (1oz) milk powder
5g (1 rounded teaspoon) dried yeast
750ml (1¼ pints) cold water
2 beaten eggs

Combine the flour, salt, fat, and milk powder. Dissolve the yeast in the water, make a well in the flour mixture and pour in the yeast-water. Knead the dough until it is smooth and pliable; this may take as long as 10 minutes.

The dough must then be left, wrapped in polythene for about an hour. It will not rise much because of the low yeast content.

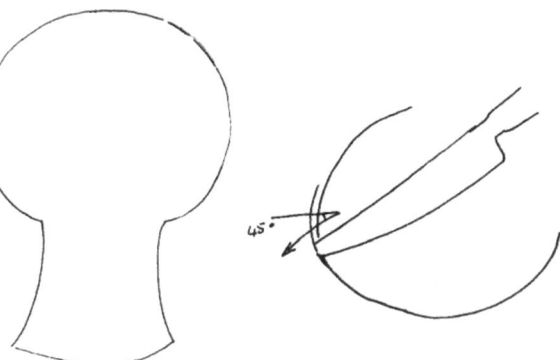

To form the dough into the wheatsheaf shape, first draw a template, for this amount of dough, about 19cm (7½") tall, 22cm (9") at the widest part of the head.

Roll out all of the dough into a rectangular shape, just larger than the template. Place the template on the dough and cut around it at a 45 degree angle. If the dough is cut straight it will turn under when baked.

Keep the remaining dough wrapped in polythene to prevent from forming a skin.

Place the base on a clean, lightly greased baking tray. Brush the dough with water to prevent a skin forming. Use a fork to lightly prick the surface of the base.

Next from thin strands of dough about 5mm (¼") in diameter and about 18cm (7") long to represent the stalks of wheat. These are laid on the base, some may be broken in half or slightly overlapping.

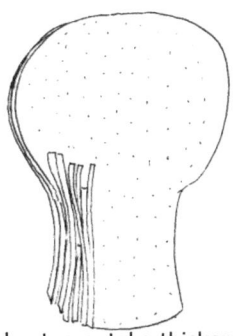

To make the wheatears, take thicker strands of dough. Place a strand of dough on the table, and make diagonal cuts 5mm (¼") in length into it at regular intervals, working from top to bottom. Roll the strand very slightly and repeat the process. Roll once more and repeat again.

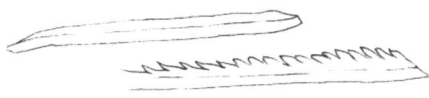

Thus the strip of dough has been cut into three sides. Cut the strip into shorter pieces to form the wheat heads. Make enough to cover the head of the base.

Place the ears of wheat on the head of the base, building up from the outside inwards and from the bottom working upwards. The ears should overlap slightly and be placed randomly. For the ties, make a three-strand plait and cut it in half. Tuck one end of each piece under the edge of the loaf at the waist. Bring the plaits together in the middle and overlap them as shown. If any dough is left over it could be used to make a little mouse.

Bake in a moderate oven Gas mark 6/200C/400F, for one hour. Check from time to time that the loaf is not browning too quickly; if it is, turn the oven down.

When the loaf looks the right, wheatsheaf colour, remove from the oven and allow to cool.

Scented Vinegar

This is a simple gift that can be made for a friend or for someone who has been ill or to keep for yourself. Fresh chrysanthemums can be eaten with salads or used in cooking. Be sure you do not use ones that have been cultivated with chemicals.

You will need
- decorative container with secure lid
- freshly picked chrysanthemum heads
- cider vinegar
- ribbon

This is very simple. Just drop the flower heads into the jar and pour warm cider vinegar onto it, secure the lid and add a ribbon for decoration.

Rain Stick

You will need
- sturdy cardboard cylinder
- flat headed nails
- hammer
- dried lentils, rice or seeds
- paint
- tape

Carefully hammer the nails into the tube. The length of the nails should be slightly smaller than the diameter of the cylinder. Remember that the lentils have to sift through the nails. If the tube has a lid use this to seal otherwise use the tape to seal one end of the tube securely.

Pour in the lentils and then cover the open end of the tube with your hand and turn the stick over to check the sound. Add more or take out some of the lentils until you are happy with the sound. Seal up the open end.

Decorate your stick with paint or you may like to use decoupage. Add wool, thread and ribbons if desired.

Apple Wreath

The circle is a sacred shape, symbolising the earth, the moon and the sacred circle of life, death and rebirth. A wreath can honour the gate to a new season and many different materials can be used. In this example I have suggested apples.

You will need
- apples
- sharp knife
- card
- glue
- cinnamon
- ribbon
- wire for hanging

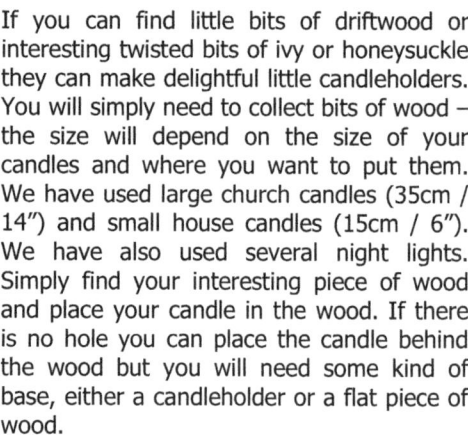

Slice the apples into 2mm (1/8th") slices and dry them in a very low oven.

Cut out a circle of card (or you could buy a wreath base) and, when the apple slices are really dry, glue them to the base. For this you could also use florist's wire.

Add some sticks of cinnamon and a bow of ribbon if you want to. Attach a ring of wire to the back for hanging.

Driftwood Candle Holders

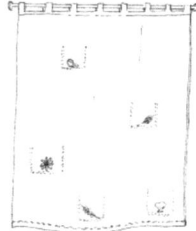

If you can find little bits of driftwood or interesting twisted bits of ivy or honeysuckle they can make delightful little candleholders. You will simply need to collect bits of wood – the size will depend on the size of your candles and where you want to put them. We have used large church candles (35cm / 14") and small house candles (15cm / 6"). We have also used several night lights. Simply find your interesting piece of wood and place your candle in the wood. If there is no hole you can place the candle behind the wood but you will need some kind of base, either a candleholder or a flat piece of wood.

Decorated Curtains

If you have collected dried leaves or heads of barley and corn or pressed flowers you may like to make a curtain out of muslin. You can use more substantial curtain material but with muslin the light shines through and makes your collected items look so pretty.

Make the curtain a double thickness and machine sew a square around the item to form a pocket. (See illustration).

You can also use this idea with bathroom curtains using shells, seaweed and other seaside items.

Vegetable Stroganoff

This is one of my favourite dishes, which is so enjoyable at this time of year when there are so many wonderful vegetables about.

a selection of fresh vegetables chopped
 into similar size pieces.
cashews or cashew pieces (I use about
 a small mug full – about 1½ cups)
the same amount of filtered water
225g/8ozs chopped mushrooms
juice of 1 lemon
1 medium onion, chopped finely
2 teaspoons vegetable bouillon powder
 (more if you want)
¼ teaspoon dill weed

To make the sauce, grind the nuts in a liquidiser, then add the water and mix into a creamy consistency.
Sauté the mushrooms and onion in oil until the onion is translucent. Add the nut cream, juice of lemon, vegetable bouillon powder and dill weed and cook very slowly.
Lightly steam the vegetables so that they do not loose their colour and place in a large dish.
Pour the sauce over them and serve immediately. You may like to add a sprinkling of paprika.

Light Vegetable Curry

225g/8ozs natural yoghurt
50g/2 ozs creamed coconut
1½ teaspoons garam masala
1 teaspoon chilli powder
1 teaspoon ginger pulp
1 teaspoon garlic pulp
¼ teaspoon turmeric
¼ teaspoon cumin seeds
¼ teaspoon ground cardamom
1 teaspoon salt
50g/2 ozs butter
2 tablespoons oil

2 onions diced
mixed fresh vegetables, cut into similar
 sized pieces
1 tablespoon fresh coriander
3 tablespoons single cream

Whisk the yoghurt and coconut then add the garam masala, chilli, ginger, garlic, turmeric, cumin seeds, cardamom and salt. Set this mixture aside.
Lightly steam the vegetables. While these are cooking, Heat the butter and oil in a heavy pot and brown the onions. Add the yoghurt mixture and cook for 2 minutes, stirring all the time.

Cheese Jacks

These are a real favourite with family and friends. The taste is unexpected as the finished result looks something like the sweet flap jacks.

150g/6ozs butter
3 eggs, beaten
750g/1lb 8ozs cheese
625g/1lb 4ozs porridge oats
1 teaspoon fresh rosemary, crushed
salt and pepper to taste
½ teaspoon mustard (optional)

Grease a shallow 8" square tin Melt the butter, remove from the heat and add the eggs and cheese. Add the oats and rosemary and press into the baking tray.
Cook on Gas mark 4/350F/180C for 20 – 30 minutes or until golden brown.

Song for Lammas

Gather Gather In

H.Royall

Gol _den heads of corn are___ hea___vy, Sac_red Moth_er smiles.

Now for har_vest here is___ plen_ty, Gath_er gath_er in.

Autumn Equinox
Story Time

AUTUMNAL EQUINOX or MABON
(22nd – 23rd September)

Now the days turn colder and we feel as though we need to build a warm nest and curl up in it even though we are not hibernating animals. The Autumnal Equinox is a time of balance when the days will begin to lose their power to the dominion of the night. We give thanks for the harvest and say goodbye to the strength of the sun. From now on the days will get shorter and preparations need to be made for the coming winter.

The harvest of the hedgerows is ready for picking; crab apple, blackberries (until the end of September), elderberries and rowan, rose hips, nuts, plums and sloes. What a good opportunity to gather the wild harvest and make preserves and potions for the months to come. A favourite of ours is sloe gin, and for the children the first blackberry pie is always a real treat.

Autumn can be a time for clearing out again, although in our house it tends to be a time for collecting dried leaves, conkers and nuts to make things and decorate the house with! One year we stayed with a Jewish friend of ours who told us of the wonders of mushroom picking.

It is always good to use the seasons to help us clear the clutter that accumulates so easily – a neglected drawer or cupboard, unfinished projects and things that we will never complete. Let the season help you to be part of the great pattern, joining those who farm the land as we prepare for winter with an ordered and wholesome living space.

The birds are not forgotten either. Seeds can be collected to feed them through the barren months when food in the wild is hard to find.

This is a time for balancing games, for gatherings that remind us of the natural balance and interdependence of male and female. Autumn is also a time of gathering, not just the bounty of the countryside but of our own achievements.

In the other gardens
And all up the vale,
From the autumn bonfires
See the smoke trail!

Pleasant summer over
And all the summer flowers,
The red fire blazes,
The grey smoke towers.

Sing a song of seasons!
Something bright in all,
Flowers in the summer
Fires in the fall!

'Autumn Fires' by Robert Louis Stevenson

123

Goddess for Autumn Equinox

Hecate

Hecate, the old woman, dressed in black, holds a lantern or flaming torch that lights the path from death to life and so could help Persephone find her way back from the Underworld.

Some consider her the Crone aspect of the Triple Goddess (Persephone being the Maiden and Demeter being the Mother). She has two dogs that walk by her side and she protects us from darkness and night-time fears.

Her symbols are the moon, the night, keys and healing herbs. She is often associated with cross roads and entrance-ways and at the Autumn Equinox, as we begin to move into her time of year, we can stand, as if at the crossroads, and ask for her blessing on our choice of pathway into Winter.

THE OLD WOMAN OF THE WOODS

The animals in the wood were worried.

All that summer the trees had been luscious and flourishing but now it was autumn and, instead of turning to gold, the forest was still green. Every tree waved its heavy branches full of green, silver, yellow and copper leaves and swayed in the autumn winds as if the dance was well known. But every tree that was not made to hold on to its leaves for so long was tired, as if trapped in some unnatural, timeless spell.

The animals wondered and watched. What should be done? Where would they get their nuts for the winter store? When could they make their homes in the autumn fall? When would the ground be fed?

It was the squirrels that thought of Her. "Why don't we talk to the Old Woman?" they asked the robin. "She knows what goes on in this wood as much as any of us and she listens to all the animals so she may know what is happening."

Ah yes, the Old Woman would know. There in the heart of the wood, in a little house made of the bent branches of the withy tree, lived an Old Woman. No one knew how long she had lived there or where she came from but she was always there, tending her garden, looking after any sick animal that was brave enough to come her way, and somehow beating with the very heart of the wood as if she was the heart of the wood itself.

Two of the squirrels, a robin and a slow but determined hedgehog made their way to the Old Woman's house. The robin arrived first and warned the Old Woman but waited patiently until the others had arrived before he told her what was worrying all the animals. "I have flown round and talked to the other birds and I have seen for myself. It seems to be the same all over the woods. The trees are not preparing for their long winter rest and they are tired."

The Old Woman was quiet for a while as if she would be able to hear the answer if she listened long enough and then she sighed, a deep, tired, careworn sigh. "There are many things that follow their cycle as night follows day but the trees have not prepared this break in their cycle themselves. I feel a different magic in the woods and it is confusing for it is not bad. I will go and find it. Stay and watch a while Robin, and I will return," and with these words she took her old, twisted holly staff and a large bag and went on her way through the woods to see what she would find.

On she went all that day and into the evening. The winds whipped the tops of the trees whispering their caution and a light frost turned the edge of the air to metal but the Old Woman found nothing but the tired trees as she wandered on. Soon she would be at the edge of the wood and instinct told her that the problem lay deeper. At last she came to one of her favourite trees that she very rarely ventured out to see. She sat down at the foot of the small but sturdy rowan tree and took from her bag a small bottle. She carefully tipped out several drops of a greenish liquid at the foot of the tree and then waited. For some time she waited and then, from somewhere deep at the heart of the little tree she felt a shudder.

"What is it my dear Rowan, stout heart, protector, friend?" she asked.

"I am heavy, so heavy." the tree whispered. "My berries that are such a delight to me in the dancing time are still here in my give away time. The birds don't want them, they know this is wrong, so wrong, and I can do nothing. I am so tired by root and branch I am so tired," and the little tree sighed and was quiet.

"Where is this magic that keeps you?" asked the Old Woman gently. There was a long pause as they listened to the wind and then the Rowan tree whispered, "It is here in the woods. It is in the apple grove where the fairies play. It will not go away."

The Old Woman placed her old, gnarled hand on the Rowan's trunk and thanked her and, picking up her staff and bag went on her way to the apple grove. It was not too far into the woods but in summer it was the most beautiful part of the wood, with the gentle blossoms followed by shiny round fruits that many of the animals delighted in and sometimes children came, taking handfuls of apples home with them.

It was not long before the Old Woman came in sight of the grove and it was as she had expected. The old, twisted trees stood in a circle each loaded with branches heavy and full of shining green and red apples. Stepping into the grove she saw a sight that took her by surprise. There sat a beautiful young woman. Long golden hair falling over her shoulders, a long green dress tucked up around her, she kneeled under one of the trees chanting a simple but compelling chant about the beauty of summer and the wholeness of the earth. She stopped when she saw the old woman and beckoned her over to sit with her.

"Old Woman, you are welcome. Isn't this the most wonderful of woods and the most plentiful of groves?" she asked.

"It is indeed," replied the Old Woman.

"Then, if you have time, come and sit with me and share my food and let me tell you a secret that fills me with such pleasure I am sure you will be pleased with it too." And the young woman proceeded to tell the Old Woman how she had learned about the chanting spell she was using on the trees of the woods to keep all things constant summer. "For think how cold people become in winter and how sad the trees look without their rich covering of beautiful leaves. Remember how happy people are in the warm summer months and how unhappy they become when it is cold and miserable. I have decided to help them and make all things remain summer with my magic and who knows, I may be able to find the answer to everlasting life and the problem of death itself! If you like you can stay with me here and I will look after you."

"That is very kind of you and in return I will tell you stories."

"Ah, that will be just fine for it can be lonely in the woods with no-one to talk to."

Then the Old Woman said, "First of all you must listen with all of your body and mind for my stories are stories of the heart." The young woman stopped humming her spells for a moment and settled herself down to listen, for the Old Woman had a way with her that made the young woman want to be still and make the most of what she would hear. Then the Old Woman spoke of seasons, and how each time is precious. She spoke of the cycle of life, death and life again. She told the story of Inanna, and Persephone and how the darkness was all part of the whole. She told stories of the apple tree and the rowan tree and the give away times and the trusting times. She told stories of the wonder and dignity of death and life and the joy of walking in Avalon.

As she spoke the young woman listened and breathed in a different magic and as her chanting magic had stopped the trees slowly, slowly began to turn golden brown and fiery reds and pinks all around her. Grateful branches gently shed their leaves and felt the lightness of their branches as if they could breath again after a long period of suffocating. All over the woods autumn crept in and the animals knew that the Old Woman had got to the heart of the problem and was healing the keeping magic.

When she had finished her stories the young woman was silent for a long time.
"Am I wrong," she asked at last, "to try to keep hold of summer when summer is so beautiful?"
"Look around you," said the Old Woman, "See how beautiful autumn is."
And then the young woman wept.

The Old Woman held her in her arms and rocked her until her crying ceased and then said gently, "It is not the summer you mourn is it my daughter?" And then the young woman told her how her young daughter had died and how utterly sad it was and how she could not understand it, it should not have happened and somehow, if she could only find the secret of life over death she could save others from the heart break of losing a loved one.

The Old Woman let the young woman talk about her child for a while and then told her of the beauty of Avalon and how every one who walked there was healed and blessed and happy. It was each person's reward for walking on this earth for a while. The young woman seemed a little comforted but then she asked, "But what about me? I am left sad and empty and alone."
"How can you be alone when there is work to do? Come with me daughter and I will teach you of your work." and so the young woman went with the Old Woman who seemed to know how to comfort just by being present and the two of them lived for a long time in the forest. The young woman learned all about the natural cycles of the earth and of the soul and one day she knew it was time for the Old Woman to leave them.
"I am older than Time Herself. I have had many names and many seasons and now it is time for me to go."
"Oh but I will be so lonely, you cannot leave me."
"Would you have me stay in summer all my life and never enjoy my autumn, my trusting time or my winter, my resting time? And would you never let me walk in Avalon and rest in my renewing time? Besides, who said I would leave you? Look at the trees, listen to their stories and you will hear my voice. Look after the earth and you will have plenty to do while I am gone." And the Old Woman smiled as she watched the young woman remembering the time of constant summer when they had met.
"Then I will come some of the way with you to Avalon and see you safely on your journey."

It is said that the young woman is still there, only now she is an Old Woman and cares for the earth and lives in the heart of the wood, in a little house made of the bent branches of the withy tree. No one knows quite how long she has lived there or where she came from but it is as if she has always been there, tending her garden, looking after any sick animal that is brave enough to come her way, specialising in any who are ready for death and the long journey to Avalon and somehow beating with the very heart of the wood as if she was the heart of the wood itself.

THINGS TO DO

Story Time

Stories on long car journeys, on walks into town, around a fire in the evenings – what could be nicer? Stories have always been part of our family life as I am a storyteller and my daughter, at a very early age, learned how to tell a good story. She would much rather I tell them but she is very good with little children and can keep them happy for long periods with her skill at creating a wonderful magical atmosphere.

We are very fond of what I call 'walking stories'. These are stories we make up as we walk along. We start our stories by setting the scene and introducing the main character/s. Then something happens to them and then they solve the problem/situation. Sometimes I tell one with a moral but my daughter got wise to those very quickly and asks me to tell her stories 'without a lesson in!' I sometimes ask her to tell me who it's about and what happens and then I weave a story around what ideas she's come up with. Sometimes I use what I see around me and put them into the story. Sometimes I use things that have happened or are happening to us. So, for example, if we were walking to town by the river I might start the story by saying ... 'Once, in a land far away, there was a swift flowing river. Trees grew by the side and an old willow hung its head sleepily over the dancing water...'

As I see different things / animals / people, I might incorporate them into the story. Once we saw a most beautiful cloud formation and so I told her a story about a land behind the clouds and recently we were walking home along by the canal and we saw some Old Man's Beard growing over a hedge, so I started a story about an old wizard who had been turned into this Old Man's Beard and how a young girl came to rescue him.

The stories can be therapeutic, educational, moral, funny, or just plain nonsense. It's great fun and as the evenings draw in somehow the magic of a story becomes easier to create.

Meditation

As evenings draw in and become darker it is a good time to encourage the family group to come together for quiet meditation or visualisations, or just to relax and let your mind drift comfortably. (You may like to guide your thoughts to something positive and relaxing! – Mark Twain was once asked if he wouldn't like to go off on holiday. He replied, "I'd like to, if only I didn't have to take that fella Mark Twain with me.")

The act of meditation has been used for centuries and is a way of helping us clear a path through the forest in order to walk on ahead.

When we encourage children or indeed anyone to meditate we are doing them a great service. If we experience peace within our own heart, within our own self, we are more likely to bring peace to those around us. Experiencing inner harmony and peace will enhance many of the wonderful gifts we have.

Meditation is a state of poised, directed concentration, a time of stilling the mind and discovering the true self. It is a time of sitting quietly and doing nothing, when the mind is held clear and still and free from losing itself in thinking. Imagine a glass of homemade apple juice. If the glass has been shaken or the juice freshly poured it will look cloudy and unappetising. When the glass is left to stand for a while the sediment settles and the juice will be clear and refreshing. In meditation we try to imitate the glass of apple juice, allowing our minds to settle.

There are many ways of encouraging children and young people to meditate. You may be experienced at this and will be at ease using your own methods. My favourite one is to sit comfortably with a child or group making sure the back is as straight as possible, the shoulders relaxed and the head balancing comfortably enjoying it's own height. (If you want to know how to sit with the correct posture look at a baby who has learned to sit up on her own.) Begin by listening to the breathing, slowing down if necessary and then lead the children through a relaxation - we often imagine a star over the head with light gently falling down over the body, relaxing the body as it goes down. We follow this by asking the children to imagine they are in a most beautiful garden, sitting comfortably, and that everything in the garden loves them. Rest there for about 5 to 10 minutes then bring them gently out and ask them to open their eyes softly. We then talk for a while about how we felt or what we saw.

Encouraging children (and adults) to draw how they are feeling can be difficult, but the results are so spectacular that it is worth persevering.

Have large sheets of paper ready and a variety of different colours and types of crayons - pastel, pencil, wax, or felt-tips. Ask the group to sit quietly for a moment. Ask them to tune into their feelings. If the feeling had a colour what would it be? Do your feelings have a shape? Draw your feelings on a piece of paper - let your hand take you where your feelings want to go.

Use your dominant hand or your non-dominant hand. Do several drawings; see how the pictures change as your feelings change.

This exercise can be used as a meditation – play quiet music in the background if you want to, but be aware that the music may influence their feelings.

You can also use drawing to begin and end a meditation. Ask the children to draw a picture as they sit quietly before they begin their meditation. When the meditation has finished ask them to stay connected to their feelings and, with soft eyes, open their eyes gently and draw a picture of how they are feeling now.

Making A Place Peaceful

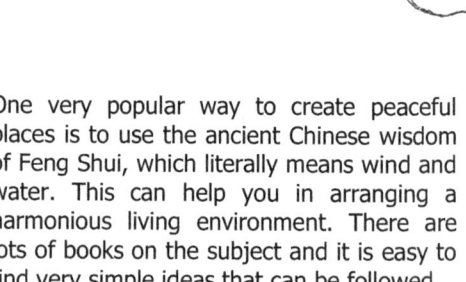

This is a lovely thing to do. You will end with something in your environment, or someone else's that creates peace or a peaceful feeling. You could choose a garden or part of a garden, a room or a part of a room or a space in your own home. You could even choose a window or a window box. Be as creative and inspired as you like with this one.

One very popular way to create peaceful places is to use the ancient Chinese wisdom of Feng Shui, which literally means wind and water. This can help you in arranging a harmonious living environment. There are lots of books on the subject and it is easy to find very simple ideas that can be followed.

Once you have chosen the place you want to work on, get to know the feel of it. Try to enhance the peaceful aspects that are there already. Think of objects and things that make you feel peaceful, such as water, stones, flowers or music, and work out which ones will suit the area you have chosen. Make sure that, if you have chosen a shared area, that the other people using it will also find the things that you have chosen peaceful. Arrange your objects, if you have any, in the way that seems to bring about the most peaceful feeling and atmosphere.

Here are some ideas -

- ✷ wind catchers made of silk or ribbon
- ✷ a sitting Goddess, Buddha or other figure
- ✷ mirrors
- ✷ wind chimes if not too windy
- ✷ coloured glass
- ✷ a beautiful poem or words
- ✷ a picture or photograph
- ✷ soft colours
- ✷ draped muslin
- ✷ plants
- ✷ water

Walk To the Hills

At the Autumn Equinox, when the day and night are the same and the veil between the worlds is thin, it is a good time to walk up to the hills at sunset. It is often still warm and the sky can be very beautiful. A late picnic is fun with children and all sorts of adventures can be enjoyed as it gets dark.

Green Man and Goblins

If the weather allows this is a great game to play in a slightly wooded area. Pick several adults or older children to be the Green Man and Goblins. (The Green Man is traditionally dressed in all green leaves and blends in to the woods.) They can be dressed up to fit their role and need to be equipped with a variety of noisemakers such as whistles, tin cans etc. They hide ready to catch or liven things up for anyone they meet. (Make sure no one else is innocently walking through the part of wood that you have chosen to play in!). The idea of the game is for the children (and adults if they want to join in) to make their way to safety through a forest (or whatever area you have chosen) infested with goblins.

Before entering the woods, each child is given four beans. Each time she is caught, the goblin demands one of her beans. She must duly hand over the bean and return to the starting line to try again. If she loses all her beans, it is all right to give her more. Players returning to the start should go around the outside of the playing area, to avoid confusing the goblins.

When the players are assembled and ready, call out to the goblins to make some noise to let everyone know if they are out there. The ensuing noise will add greatly to the excitement.

You can chose to have your Green Man as a help or to be as wild as the goblins. The Green Man has also been called the Lord of Growing Things, Jack-In-The-Green, Robin Goodfellow and Robin Hood. He is the son of Pan, the Greek god of all wild things.

Who Goes There?

This is a game for the dark. Choose a quiet area or pathway. The watcher sits in the middle of the 'road' with his eyes closed and a torch in his hand. The other players line up at a point some distance away. Then several players try to stalk past him together and reach a base (an area decided beforehand.) If the watcher hears anything, he shines his light in that direction. Anyone the light touches must freeze. (No wild sweeping of the light around!) The first to pass the watcher and reach base becomes the new watcher.

'Being' Walks

For this you will need a young child to accompany you, although you may be able to do it with older children or adults if you have not lost the ability! Take a walk anywhere you want to go and just stop to look at what is around you. The small child will be interested in everything around, especially the things on his or her level and lower. Take time to look 'with new eyes' at all that you see.

When we were in Spain on holiday one year, my friend, Issy, took my daughter for a walk. He commented on how interesting it was for him looking at things that were very familiar but that were new to my daughter. He felt like he was looking at things for the first time.

Conkerwebs

You will need
- a shiny chestnut
- barbecue-skewers or cocktail sticks
- coloured wool
- thread for hanging
- a large needle or matchstick

With the needle or matchstick make at least seven holes round the chestnut. Then insert a cocktail stick or barbecue-skewer depending on the size you require.
Select a coloured wool, tie one end on to one of the sticks and press the wool hard against the chestnut. Lead the wool from stick to stick, and round each stick in the

same way as for Eyes of Light (page 57). Continue until a colour strip becomes evident. Cut the wool, and tie on another colour and continue. Make the knots as small as possible and see that they lie at the back of the web. You can have the nice smooth round side of the conkerweb as the front or you may like the ribs to show. Finish by tying the wool onto one of the sticks.
You can vary this by using one colour only and leaving a space between each round. This makes it look like a beautiful spider web.

Dried Leaves

Collect different coloured and shaped leaves and press them in-between pages of a large book, like a telephone directory, or put them between pieces of clean paper and put several heavy books on top of them.
If your leaves curl up when they are dry before you have had time to press them soak them in water for a few hours and then press them as above.
Not all leaves lend themselves to drying. Some lose their colour and others look better when left to dry naturally, like oak for example.
When they are dry you can use them as decorations for things like notepaper, or picture frames. At this time of year we are beginning to collect things that we may be able to use to make Solstice presents or even to use on our Winter Solstice or Christmas cards.

Leaf Skeletons

Leaf skeletons are made by removing all the soft material from a leaf, leaving only the veins. There are several ways of making leaf skeletons, one using cabbage leaves boiled in water. I do not use this one because it is very smelly and takes a week. If you do not like the idea of using soda you will need to put your leaves into cabbage water (about six large cabbage leaves to 2 pints water – simmered for half an hour and left to cool) and leave them there for a week until the vegetable matter has softened. Rinse them very gently in clear water and use a soft bristled paintbrush to dislodge any remaining leaf material. For the soda method -

You will need
- washing soda
- water
- saucepan
- clean newspaper
- soft bristled paint brush

Dissolve a dessertspoonful of soda to each pint of water, heat to below boiling point, remove from the heat and soak the leaves for about an hour. Brush away the rotting material. Be careful not to get the soda in the eyes or the skin.
Place the leaf skeleton on a piece of clean newspaper and leave in an airing cupboard to dry.

Sun Wheel for Summers End

The sun wheel can be made with rowan or willow branches, vervain and rue. Together they will keep negativity away, protect you from evil influences and bring health to all

the occupants of your home throughout the winter.

You will need
- long thin rowan or willow branches soaked overnight (preferably during a waning moon for banishing).
- red thread (the colour of life)
- gold ribbon (for sunlight)
- vervain
- rue (be aware that some people have a strong allergic reaction to touching rue.)

Soak the rowan or willow branches overnight in water. Fashion these into a circle with an equidistant cross in the centre representing the four major points of the year. Bind the ends securely with the red thread. Let the branches dry until the following full moon. Then decorate the circle with vervain, rue and golden ribbons.

A Crown Of Leaves

You will need
- large autumn leaves
- sticky tape (optional)

Cut off the stems and keep them. Lay one leaf partly over another and press a stem through them both to pin them together. Continue until the crown has reached the desired length. If necessary strengthen the crown by sticking a strip of sticky tape along the inside. Finally pin the two ends together and the crown is finished.

Sort out your Seeds

Now is the time to sort out any seeds you may want to use next spring. One year, for our Winter Solstice presents, our friend Leslie gave us a beautiful bouquet of evergreen branches from her garden with lovely dried poppy heads in it. Some people don't like poppies in their garden because they run wild but our garden is made up of lots of pots so they are easy to keep in order. If you are thinking of making a butterfly garden (see page 62) you may like to see what seeds you can prepare for this.

Wild Harvest

Late September is a good time to start looking for nuts to eat. You need to eat hazel nuts when they are fully ripe to enjoy the almost fishy flavour of the brown cobs. The trouble is you have to get to them before the squirrels. Remember, if you do get lucky and find some, don't take too many, as the wild animals will want some too. If you do see some, in bunches of two or three, go for them very carefully as they fall from their husks easily.

In October and November you will find sweet chestnuts, a really scrummy nut, which is wonderful roasted. Don't confuse this one with the horse chestnuts, whose inedible conkers look very similar inside their spiny husks.

If you decide to go out and sample the wild harvest at any time of year take a book with you so that you don't make any mistakes and eat something that will do you harm. Better still, take someone who knows all about finding food in the wild. A good book to get is 'Food For Free' by Richard Mabey.

Autumn Table Setting

For a special look give your table a natural autumn setting by collecting oak leaves. Some green, if you can still find them, some brown and some painted gold.

Tablecloth and napkins

You will need
- beige tablecloth if you have one or a paper tablecloth
- napkins of same material or paper

serviettes
- oak leaf
- potato
- paper
- sharp knife
- gold fabric paint
- paint brush
- old towel

Choose a suitable leaf to use as a guide. Place it on the paper, draw round it and cut it out.
Cut the potato in half and place the paper leaf on the flat edge. Cut around it with the sharp knife.
Cut the potato into a rectangular shape around the leaf. Cut a detail such as a vein into the leaf.
Brush gold paint onto the cut leaf pattern, avoiding the carved-out detail.
Place an old towel under the tablecloth; press the potato on to the cloth to print. Either use a regular pattern or place the leaf prints at random.

Table decoration

In the centre of your table add a bowl or vase of oak leaves of different colours. Or you could use the oak ring (see page 27) with a candle in the centre.

Pot Luck Suppers

This is a lovely time of year to gather your friends around and invite them to bring some food to share. There are all sorts of ways to do this depending on your circumstances and inclination. You could ask everyone to bring a vegetable to put into a stew pot and a fruit to put into the fruit salad, or ask each one to bring a different course, or ask everyone to bring anything they like, or chose a theme such as a colour, an ingredient or style. It is always fun and there is always lots left over. People can take home what is left over of their own or take someone else's.

Tomato and Red Pepper Soup

We were given this when we were in Spain last autumn. It was cooked in a wonderful Spanish kitchen by a woman from Yorkshire!

3 red peppers, cored and deseeded
1kg (2lbs) ripe tomatoes, halved and
   deseeded
2 red onions quartered
2 garlic cloves, peeled
2 tablespoons tomato purée
1.25 litres (2 pints) vegetable stock
salt and black pepper
3 tablespoons single cream

Preheat the oven to Gas 6 / 400C/200F. Place the peppers, tomatoes, onion and garlic in a roasting tin and bake in the oven for 15 – 20 minutes until the pepper skins have blistered.
Allow to cool slightly, then remove the skins from the peppers, tomatoes and onions and place in a food processor with the garlic, tomato purée and 150ml (¼ pint) of the vegetable stock.
Blend the vegetable mixture until smooth, then pour into a large pan and add the remaining stock, salt and pepper. Bring to the boil and simmer for 15 minutes.
Serve with a swirl of cream.

Song for Autumn
Golden Leaves

H.Royall

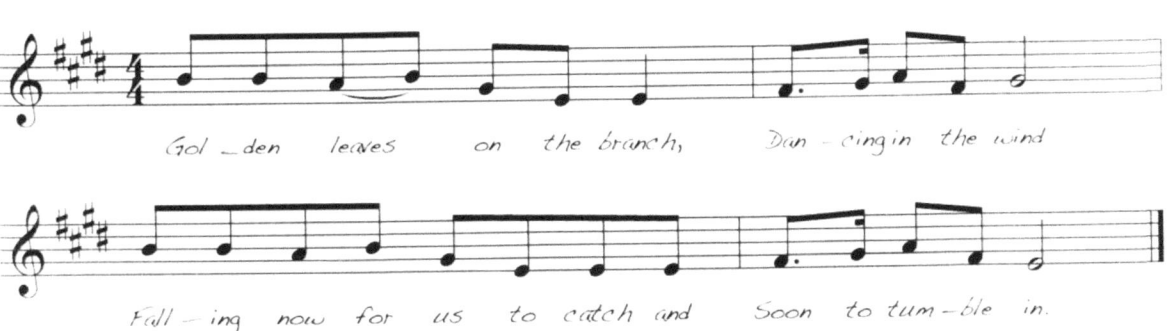

Gol – den leaves on the branch, Dan – cing in the wind

Fall – ing now for us to catch and Soon to tum – ble in.

FEEL THE JOY

Come, take a walk in the fields and witness
The abundance of life, the beauty, the
peace.
Sit under an oak tree and ponder life's
mysteries.
For a while let your cares blow away with
the breeze

See the crows swooping to hassle the
buzzard
As he rises on thermals with effortless ease.
And wander into the scented woodland
With a carpet of bluebells under the trees.
Come take a stroll in the field of buttercups
As the morning sunshine blesses the day.
Hear the dawn chorus and watch for the fox
As little brown rabbits hop out of harm's
way.

Stroll to a viewpoint, with birds singing gaily.
Gather some strawberries warmed by the
sun.
Lie in the grass and study the creatures,
Intent on a purpose - every one.
As night scented flowers give the air
sweetness
And daytime life settles with the last
blackbird's cry,
Sit in the stillness, watching bats feeding,
And wait for the badgers to snuffle right by.

Climb up The Peak and gaze at the
landscape
Then enter the beech woods, turned gold
and red.
Catch falling leaves as they flutter and
tumble,
Whilst squirrels hide nuts for long months
ahead.
Stay out when dark clouds gather low on the
skyline
And an eerie quiet descends all around.
Feel rain pelt your face, the wind pound
your body,
Submit to the storm: know its power, its
sound.

When a strange morning brightness shines
through the curtains,
Know there has dawned a most special day.
Come out in the snow, come sledging, build
snowmen:
Finding, within you, the child: just play.

Return in the moonlight to untrodden
pathways
Through trees, majestic, with branches laid
low.
The world seems at peace: such perfection
and beauty
And silence save the creak of steps in the
snow.

Remember the past, imagine the future
But never forget that today life is real.
Each season, each day, may you find what is
special
And may you too feel the joy I feel.

Sandra Hosler, Spring 2002

THE BEGINNING

And so the process of birth, growth, death and rebirth is played out, and the wheel turns on and on. Find your own myths and symbols to represent your wheel, discover your own names for the different stages of the moon and for each moon month. Allow yourself to grow and change as you discover more of what Mother Earth wants to teach you and live with that deep respect and love for all that is living. Read books that are inspiring, walk in places that fill you with joy. Talk to people who make your heart sing and most of all work on love, as often and as much as you can.

This book is not about how to live your life or how to bring up your children, it is not about how to celebrate the seasons – it is about finding your own way of doing these things. I have recorded some of the ideas I have tried out over the years with my family and I encourage you to go and do the same.

May you find joy.

> **"I who am the beauty of the green earth and the white moon among the stars and the mysteries of the waters, I call upon your soul to arise and come unto me.**
> For I am the soul of nature that gives life to the universe. From Me all things proceed and unto Me they will return. Let my worship be in the heart that rejoices, for behold, all acts of love and pleasure are My rituals – Let there be beauty and strength, power and compassion, honour and humility, mirth and reverence within you.
> And you who seek to know Me, know that your seeking and yearning will avail you not, unless you know the mystery: for if that which you seek, you find not within yourself, you will never find it without. For behold, I have been with you from the beginning, and I am that which is attained at the end of desire."
>
> *Traditional by Doreen Valiente, as adapted by Starhawk*

BIBLIOGRAPHY

Bain, George - **Celtic Art** – Constable 0 09 461830 5

Berger, Thomas–**The Christmas Craft Book** – Floris Books

Berger,Thomas and Petra – **The Easter Craft Book** – Floris Books 0 86315 161 2

Capacchione, Lucia – **The Picture of Health** – Newcastle Publishing

Brodie, Jan **Earth Dance** –– Capall Bann Publishing 1 898307 30 5

Carey, Diana, Judy Large, **Festivals Family and Food** –– Hawthorn Press 0 950 7026 3X

Chanin, Michael **Grandfather Four Winds and Rising Moon** – Starseed Press 0 915811 47 2

Carol, Christ **Rebirth of the Goddess** –– Addison Wesley 0201 14398 4

Cornell, Joseph Bharat **Sharing Nature With Children** –– Exely Publications 1 85015 137 7

Joseph, Cornell **Listening To Nature** –– Exley 1 85015 095 8

Deadman, Peter, Karen Betteridge, – **Nature's Foods** – Unicorn Bookshop 85659 012 6

Fontana, David and Ingrid Slack – **Teaching Meditation To Children** – Element 1 86204 0184

Green, Marian **A Witch Alone** – The Aquarian Press 1 85538 112 5

Hanh, Thich Nhat – **The Sun My Heart** –– Rider 0 7126 5422 4

Holden, Edith – **The Country Diary of an Edwardian Lady** – Michael Joseph 0 7181 1581 3

Roberts, Wendy Hunter – **Celebrating Her** – The Pilgrim Press 0 8298 1258 X

Jones, Ron – **The Unusual World Records Book** –– (1201 Stanyan Street, San Francisco, CA 94117)

Kenton, Lesley – **The Biogenic Diet** –– Arrow Books 0 09 950740 4

Kindred, Glennie – **The Earths Cycle of Celebration and The Sacred Tree** – Earthkind (c/o 3 Danbury Mount, Sherwood, Nottingham NG5 4BL)

Mabey, Richard – **Food For Free** –– Peerage Books 1 85052 052 6

Mantin, Ruth,– **Can Goddesses Travel With Nomads and Cyborgs**? Feminist Thealogies in a Postmodern Context – Feminist Theology No 26 Jan 2001 ISSN 0966 7350

Margetts, Martina (ed.) – **Classic Crafts** – Guild Publishing

Moorey, Theresa – **Spellbound** – Rider 0 71 261253 X

Morton, Nelle – **The Journey Is Home** – Beacon Press 0 8070 1133 9

O'Conner, Joseph, John Seymour **Introducing NLP Neuro-Linguistic Programming** – Harper Element 97818 553 83449

Raphael, Melissa - **Introducing Thealogy** – Pilgrim Press/United Church Press- 08298 137 99

Serith, Ceisiwr – **The Pagan Family** – Llewellyn Publications 0 87542 210 1

Slade, Paddy – **Natural Magic** – Hamlyn 0 600 57064 9

Solomonsen, Jone – **Enchanted Feminism** – Routledge (Religion and Gender) 0 415 22393 8

Starhawk etc – **Circle Round** – Bantam Books 0553 37805 8

Starhawk – **Spiral Dance** – HarperSanFransisco 0 06 250814 8

Telesco, Patricia – **Seasons of the Sun** – Samuel Weiser 0 87728 872 0

Handbook of Country Crafts – AA Drive Publications Ltd

Womanguides – Beacon Press 0 8070 1203 3

The Complete Works of Shakespeare – Cambridge University Press

The Natural Garden Book – Gaia Books Ltd 1 85675 056 6